Dear Rec

CW00449876

# Climb your
# S.T.A.I.R.™ of
# Self-Confidence

Wishing you
Love Light & happiness
always
Love Bernadette x

**Bernadette Sarginson**

A CIP catalogue record of this book is available from the British Library.

Published by Goldcrest Books International Ltd

www.goldcrestbooks.com

publish@goldcrestbooks.com

ISBN: 978-1-911505-33-4

**Spirit Level**
SUCCESS™ SYSTEM
SIX SECRETS OF SELF-ESTEEM

## Praise for 'Climb your S.T.A.I.R.™ of Self-Confidence'

'This book is an absolute must for anyone that wants to reduce anxiety and re-balance their life. Expertly written, full of content with do-able, brilliant techniques that can change your body, mind and energy vibration. "You cannot take someone through a door you haven't walked through yourself" and that's what makes this book so compelling as Bernadette shares her own past vulnerabilities and 'not enough-ness' and how she overcame this. As a self-kindness advocate I recommend this book to anyone that wants a more loving, kind and abundant relationship with themselves.'

**Liz Keaney – Speaker, Author, Coach**
**www.lizkeaney.com**

'The Spirit Level Success™ System is brilliant. It is crafted from profound insights into an elegant and accessible system. A practical and intelligent approach, it guides you to the heart of what it is to understand, and then achieve, your capacity for greatness.'

**Trevor Folley - ILM Level 7 Executive Coach, NLP Master Practitioner www.lindenlearning.co.uk**

'This is so much more than a book about self-confidence - it's a complete manual for living well. Written from the heart and communicated with soul, Climb Your S.T.A.I.R™ of Self-confidence has the power to help anyone who is looking for less stress, more abundance and a richer experience of life. A beautiful little book that has the power to transform lives.'

**Sophie Bennett - Keynote Speaker and Bestselling Author**
**www.sophiebennett.com**

'Climb your S.T.A.I.R.™ of Self-Confidence is invaluable, powerful, essential learning for every human being. Bernadette's powerful words read as the helpful friend we all need. I would recommend not just reading this book, but re-reading it until the key points are instilled within you. With an easy to absorb, straight forward and logical approach, it begins by creating essential, solid foundations and then builds upwards. Bernadette gently encourages you to apply the techniques and embrace the wisdom, and in doing so, you will change your life.'

**Thomas Dawson – Management Development Consultant**
**www.traininginterventions.co.uk**

'In the construction world, the spirit level is a basic but essential tool that's used to confirm when something is true, straight and aligned with the plan. The Spirit Level Success™ System is a discreet, yet powerful mind-tool that empowers you to instantly restore your self-balance, handle the curve-balls and re-establish your focus.'

**Ian Lawman – Entrepreneur and Accidental Mentor**
**www.TheAccidentalMentor.co.uk**

'The knowledge and wisdom within this brilliant little book, drawn from experience, is immense power delivered in a most gentle way. Slow down and take your time to absorb it. Let what you learn be your guide now, and in the future. You Are (most definitely) Worth It!'

**Valerie Dwyer – Success Coach, Speaker, Author**
**www.mywonderfullifecoach.co.uk**

'Climb Your S.T.A.I.R.™ of Self-confidence provides a powerful toolkit of insights and teachings, presented in a way that is easy to read and relate to. A great structure for ongoing work and reflection. I thoroughly enjoyed my journey through this book.'

**Sarah Marwick – Training & Educational Consultant**
**www.knowyourpurpose.life**

'Wow, this book is amazing. I was intrigued right from the start and just couldn't put it down. It is a complete, holistic, therapeutic and spiritual process for the ultimate advancement in empowerment. Brilliant!'

**Julie Anne Hart – Intuitive Leadership Consultant**
**www.julieannehart.com**

'This book was a wonder to read, and made me immediately want to contract with the author to write a children's version. It is the perfect time for Climb your S.T.A.I.R.™ of Self-Confidence, as the global pressure of instant social media and fake advertising is causing so much damage to so many people. 'Being enough' isn't about conformity or comparison or being a certain way, having a certain look, being the right weight, wearing the right clothes, or even having the right attitude. Being enough means it's ok to be you. You are enough. Well done Bernadette, a great tool in the self-development toolbox.'

**Neil Marwick - Educator, co-founder and Director of MiWorld Network**

'What hit me really deeply when I read this book is the humility that Bernadette brings to her work and the compassion that she shares with others. Reading the words, one feels that this work is her 'mission' to reach and teach others who are struggling with sense of self, who are struggling with low self-esteem and who really need a helping hand to get through the blocks that hold them back. You can't teach what you haven't learnt and in Climb your S.T.A.I.R.™ of Self-Confidence, Bernadette really digs deep to share with us the tools that helped her transform her life. In short it does what it says on the tin - a simple, effective, repeatable and sustainable system for reducing anxiety, and re-balancing your self-esteem and sense of self-worth. Thank you for sharing your powerful and unique system to help others be their best self.'

**Jo Soley – Your Brilliant Business Angel and Coach**
**www.josoley.com**

'When you look intently, you'll see that most successful people make it look easy. They seem to be able to get more done, have greater relationships and spend time caring about making our world a better place too.

And that's because every single one of them has a *structure* — a way of doing things that brings repeatable results every time.

Now, in this magical book, you get given such a system — one that's beautifully simple and so easy to apply. Bernadette has done amazing things to 'codify' the structure in a way that you'll love. The people around you will notice instantly. They'll see a beautiful change in you too.

This book doesn't just get you on a great path, it keeps you there too. It's a must-have for anyone seeking a life that's more fulfilling and more rewarding every second, every day and in every way.'

**Paul Dunn – Chairman Buy1Give1, TEDx Speaker and Master Presenter www.b1g1.com**

To my husband Lee, without whose unconditional love, understanding and support, this book would never have been written. I love you more with every passing day.

And my daughters Ellie and Ruby – you are my world. Your light and laughter; love, compassion and beauty from within, take my breath away.

I am so lucky to have found you all in this lifetime; you inspire me.

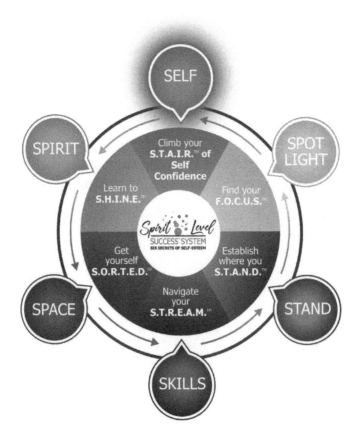

The **Spirit Level Success™ System – Six Secrets of Self-Esteem** is a complete system, and each Secret is a core component of what I believe needs to be in balance to maintain a healthy, robust core and feel good about yourself all the time – no matter what is going on in your life.

**Secret #1 – Self –** where you **Climb your S.T.A.I.R.™ of Self-Confidence** gets you there; **Secrets #2 – #6** keep you there.

Wherever 'there' is for you.

You can access resources and find out more about the complete system at **www.spiritlevelsuccess.com**

# CONTENTS

# FOREWORD

The greatest gift we have is life. And the lifeforce, our breath, our spirit, our essence is the perfection and the beauty and the magnificence of who we are.

One of the saddest things that I see and feel physically, emotionally, mindfully and spiritually is when we diminish that lifeforce, breath, spirit and essence that is ours, that is yours, that is your birth-right. That lifeforce that is the very reason you are alive on this planet.

It's been an absolute honour to read this book. And I would recommend it to anyone and everyone, because it highlights the path of returning. Returning to that natural lifeforce, breath, essence, spirit, sense of self and the beauty of you. And when you experience and begin to experience the beauty of you, you have the freedom and the abundance and the gift that being here on this amazing planet gives you.

Life is a journey, it's not a destination. And reading this book places you upon that journey. A journey of discovery, a journey of understanding, a journey of knowing who you are and the richness and pleasure of taking ownership of yourself. With loving care, with nurture, with all the ingredients that sometimes in our separation from our self we lose – compassion, care, honour, respect, values, a sense of esteem. Climb your S.T.A.I.R.™ of Self-Confidence gives you back the vital ingredients that boost your lifeforce so you can see, feel and experience your truth.

You have been blessed to find this path and to find this book. And in these pages and within these sentences and words, you will come home to you.

**Julie Anne Hart**

**Intuitive Leadership Consultant**
**www.julieannehart.com**

*For Mum and Dad*

*"How does one become a Butterfly?"*
*she asked pensively...*

*"You must want to fly so much, that
you are willing to give up being a
Caterpillar."*

**Dr Wayne Dyer**

# CHAPTER ONE

## Is this book right for you?

Are you someone who always feels great about yourself and never experiences any kind of self-doubt or low self-esteem ever?

Are you the kind of person who is perpetually rock solid, unshakeable and unwaveringly confident?

**If this is you, please, replace this book on the shelf and back away slowly. This book isn't for you.**

But before you do put it back, please have a think about who you know who may desperately need the knowledge, skills and strategies contained within these pages, and whose life may just change for the better in the most profound way, just because you cared enough to buy this for them.

Imagine what it would be like to eliminate fear. Not the normal, healthy kind of fear that is emotionally appropriate and lets you know you either need to act in some way or that you're stretching yourself beyond your comfort zone.

But the insipid, low level fear and anxiety that infiltrates every cell in your body, extinguishes your hope and joy and cripples you from the inside out.

If you have learned to live with low level anxiety and you now experience this as normal, this book is an absolute 'must read' for you and will prove to be the first essential step to reclaiming your sense of self and your mental health and well-being.

> **Do you sometimes tell yourself that everyone else is doing OK and you're the only person in the world who thinks like you, who speaks to yourself in the way you do or who feels like you do?**

How would it feel to be able to honestly and gently hold the truth that 'I am worthy and valuable' or 'I am enough', and keep your head held high no matter what?

**This book is not going to ask you to believe anything that feels uncomfortable, or suggest that you subscribe to any particular philosophy.** All it asks is that you follow the process, and let your brain and body do the rest. You do need to actively engage, and you do need to bring an open mind, a sense of curiosity and an active imagination, but you don't need to believe anything for this to work – except one thing. You simply need to believe that it is possible for you to change and for things to be different for you.

If you can take that belief with you as you read this book, then you will give yourself the absolute best chance of bringing about the change you so desperately seek.

The process isn't about spirituality, except to the extent that you want it to be. It will not be asking you to believe anything specific about Spirit, God, the  Universe, faith or whatever – other than to hold what you already believe to be true. But it is about raising your level of consciousness of who you are and how you live your life, and more specifically, it's about the relationship you have with yourself. On the inside.

If you are the kind of person who is functioning well, certainly as far as the outside world is concerned, but at times has moments of self-doubt, low self-esteem with maybe a little self-loathing thrown in for good measure, then there is wisdom within these pages that will prove invaluable for you.

Your self-esteem shouldn't be tied up with your professional status, wealth, body size or any other externally evidenced aspect of your life. But sadly, it all too often is.

Please know that wherever you are right now, this will pass. And the tools and wisdom in this book will elevate you to a position where you can simply, effectively and repeatedly re-balance your self-esteem and sense of self-worth any time, every time. Whenever you need it, whomever you are with.

Self-doubt, at points in your life, is to be expected and is completely understandable. It's part of what makes you human. But when it becomes consistent and debilitating, that's the time many people will turn to antidepressants to fix themselves. But antidepressants only treat the symptoms and not the cause. The cause lies in your thinking and your beliefs about yourself, it lies in how you speak to yourself, and the kind of questions you ask yourself when life throws its challenges at you.

Every single person in the world, to varying degrees, has moments of self-doubt and anxiety, suffering and struggle because of their own negative self-talk and self-limiting beliefs. Your self-esteem and sense of self-worth can hit rock bottom on occasions. You may even have periods of self-loathing at some point in your life. It's normal, so you are not alone. This state of emotional flux may be quite intermittent for you or it may be more consistent. Either way, you understand what it feels like to experience it. Sometimes more, sometimes less, but experience it you have.

---

I want to let you know that there are tools, techniques and strategies that you can use for yourself to mean that you can bring yourself back from that place any time and I created the Spirit Level Success™ System – Six Secrets of Self-Esteem (www.spiritlevelsuccess.com) to make this knowledge easy to understand, apply and remember, and to make it accessible to anyone who needs it.

This book is just about Secret #1.

---

You may already know that there is a strong and very specific link  between how you speak to yourself (your internal dialogue or self-talk) and how you feel (your internal 'felt' experience) and then how you behave (what you do, that other people would notice). Put simply, this means that your 'self-talk', in other words what you think about yourself, what you believe and what you say to yourself at any point, will always determine what 'state' you are in and what you achieve in your life , because it is all an inter-connected system. The good news is that when you change one part of the system, the rest of the system changes. It can't not. So when you change how you think and speak to yourself, everything else changes.

This book is not a substitute for seeking professional mental health advice and support when you really need it. It is though my hope that it can become your own self-help 'Catcher in the Rye'[1]. But instead of catching children before they lose their innocence and fall over the cliff edge into 'phoney adulthood' as in J.D. Salinger's book, you'll be able to catch yourself before falling over the edge of your own 'cliff' into low self-esteem and self-worth and a potential lifetime of addictive antidepressants.

> **Have you ever had that experience where it can sometimes feel like there is a war zone in your head, with gunfire and hand grenades going off in quick succession?**

1. Catcher in the Rye – J.D. Salinger 1951

The late Carrie Fisher once described this as 'your own internal Aleppo' in reference to a modern-day war zone, and it can feel like a relentless bombardment of criticism and haranguing about not being enough.

Do you know what it's like to sometimes feel like you're standing right on the edge of that kind of metaphorical cliff?

Behind you is the artillery and the gunfire of your internal dialogue, the horrendous way you've been speaking to yourself or interpreting life's circumstances to always mean something negative about you. When it feels like a war zone, it is hard. It is cruel. It is unkind. And it is unrelenting.

Before you is the cliff edge.

Unless you have been to that place, it can be difficult to understand what it's really like and to fully appreciate  what you need in order to change things for yourself.

Do you jump into the unknown, into the abyss, into the oblivion?

Or today do you say 'enough!' and decide that you will reclaim your power, stand upright, shoulders back, chin up and turn to face the way you've just come, with a renewed sense of your own ability not just to manage your way through the shells and bombs, but to be able to dissipate the weapons and the enemy through conscientious choices about how you want to think, feel and behave?

I have been to that place at times in my life and when I am there, everything seems so heightened, so real, so painful, so laden with suffering. And the discomfort is cumulative, so each additional vicious verbal blow from your internal dialogue layers upon everything else that has gone before, just like a line of upraised dominoes that falls predictably once the first one tips over.

Thoughts that come into your mind can be appallingly unsupportive, and are almost always self-destructive as they chip away at your self-esteem, your sense of self-worth and your sense of just being completely OK as you are.

This book will give you the tools to be able to stop the domino effect in its' tracks, and re-balance; regain your perspective; and realise how special you are, so you can turn things around and get on with living your best life.

> **If you truly, genuinely want to make a change and make things different and better and empower yourself to be able to take control and re-balance yourself any time, then Climb your S.T.A.I.R.™ of Self-Confidence right now.**

*What do you have to lose?*

This book is for you if you know what it feels like to have a temporary 'wobble' that sometimes lingers such that you struggle to see your way back. This book will help you if you are motivated to want to fix this for yourself with a simple, effective, repeatable and sustainable system which is easy to remember and apply, and will give you consistent results without the need for medication or any other external intervention.

If this resonates with you, please read this book from cover to cover and fully immerse yourself in every chapter, taking the time to connect and engage with everything that is asked of you.

No-one will ever need to know that you are doing something differently or following a specific system unless you tell them, because it all takes place on the inside; in your mind and body. So you can do this completely at your own pace, in private, in your own way and with an approach that feels completely comfortable to you.

When you can use the techniques effortlessly, because you have learned and practised them, you will be able to break the negative, downward cycle of ruminative thinking and interrupt the pattern of going over and over and over the same unhelpful destructive thoughts.

If you want things to change, you have to do something different. And I passionately believe that this book will empower you to be able to reduce your anxiety, and re-balance your self-esteem and sense of self-worth any time, every time.

> **When you feel good about yourself, you can have a different relationship with your fear and anxiety such that it completely dissipates; putting you back in the driving seat of your life.**

Success is all about managing your internal state, which is everything. What happens in the world around you and in your external environment cannot, in and of itself, affect your self-esteem and sense of well-being. The deciding factor with how things turn out is your internal emotional and cognitive responses.

What habits of thinking do you have? What assumptions do you usually and typically make about yourself and other people? Do you always tend to assume you have done something wrong when another person questions you about something you've done? How 'old' do you usually feel when you are communicating with certain specific individuals who are in your life? Do you sometimes feel like you did when you were at school?

It might possibly be that you are in the habit of chastising yourself not only for the things you have said and done, but also for decisions you have made or opportunities you didn't grasp along the road to getting where you are today.

It's normal to have doubts, fears and insecurities. It's part of what makes you human, being healthily vulnerable. But when it's so bad it cripples you into inaction – that's where the balance has tipped, and rectification is urgently needed to avoid this becoming a more serious and insidious mental health issue like anxiety or depression.

**But what can you do?**

**Where can you go for help?**

You can Climb your S.T.A.I.R.™ of Self-Confidence anywhere and any time you need a shift in your internal state. Whether you're feeling a bit low or need a little boost in confidence; it will work.

Just before a meeting or interview; before going to work or going out; or even just facing your day – it is guaranteed to get you in the best possible place for success, whatever you decide to do or achieve that day.

This book will light the way and show you how to negotiate your way back, when you feel like you're lost. And most importantly of all – to do it for yourself without the need to have anyone or anything else involved.

You really can use the techniques contained in this book anywhere, any time and in any circumstance. Even through the night, if you wake and struggle to get back to sleep. Because all you need is you. There is nothing outside of you that needs to be present or available.

Please value yourself enough to fully engage, immerse and experience each step, knowing that by doing so, it will make a world of difference to you.

You matter. Just as much as any other person out there.

You are unique. You are special.

You may not always realise and appreciate this, but it is true.

All of the time.

And I believe you can do this, even if you don't quite believe it just yet.

*"It occurs to me that without fear, I might be strong, powerful, unstoppable."*

Veronica Roth

# CHAPTER TWO

## Why would you listen to me?

Firstly, thank you for reading this book. I hope it will change your life.

I am honoured and humbled to think that the Spirit Level Success™ System – Six Secrets of Self-Esteem (www.spiritlevelsuccess.com) is fulfilling my life purpose and mission of empowering, through self-help, as many people as possible who have a daily battle with their destructive and highly critical inner demons, to be able to find a way through to feeling good about themselves when they need to, without the need for therapy or drugs, unless it is their genuine choice to follow either of those paths.

**So who am I and why might you be interested in what I've got to say?**

# My Story

*I had a very happy childhood. Generally speaking. I was a confident, cheerful child who was always smiling, certainly so in my early years. I loved school, I loved playing. We didn't have much money, but I just loved life, and everything that was great about growing up in the 1970s.*

*What I didn't know back then, was that I had a diagnosable and treatable bladder condition which was to cause me challenges of varying degrees well into my adult life, until I finally got the simple diagnosis and treatment to fix it.*

*Because of this bladder condition, I wet the bed far longer than you might expect from a bright, intelligent girl. Probably until about age 10 – way after I 'should' have stopped. I didn't understand why it kept happening, and although I was desperate, I couldn't work out how to make it stop.*

*Back in the 70s, parenting was a little different than it is today. And the way my parents dealt with my bed-wetting was the first time in my young life that I remember experiencing feeling shame. A real, deep sense of shame. For not being able to stop.*

*And for disappointing them, because I kept wetting the bed.*

*As I got older and older, and it still kept happening, the internal desperation and the shame only intensified. In equal proportions.*

*It wasn't necessarily what my parents said or did in response to the bed-wetting, but more about how I internalised what was happening to me. So I don't blame them. I love them both very dearly, and I know that they were doing their best to parent in the best way they knew how.*

*The whole experience though proved to be a catalyst that would shape how I felt about myself for many years to come.*

Can you relate to that? Is there something that happened in your own childhood that had such a profound impact on how you felt about yourself? Maybe it still does...

I'm in my midlife now and, with the benefit of hindsight, I can see that it was all a **G.I.F.T.**™ – a **G**olden **I**nsight into **F**eelings and **T**houghts. But it wasn't always that way.

*Over the years, I achieved increasing outward success and, on the surface, had a bubbly personality and an outwardly happy, successful life. But with every additional knock and negative comment that was directed at me whether from teachers or peers through my pre-teen and teenage years, it gradually stripped away at my self-esteem, and I developed the recognised condition of Social Anxiety. Not that I had that diagnosed by the way. The label would have been too much for me to bear.*

*I recall many times in social situations through my teens and twenties becoming desperate for the attention not to be on me, with cheeks burning bright red as I struggled to find my words, feeling like I was under intense scrutiny, which wasn't actually the case, but such is the power of the thoughts you tell yourself; whether or not they are true.*

*And the thing that made this such a tough burden to carry? It was my shameful, hidden secret that I tried desperately to cope with on the inside, despite my growing academic and professional success on the outside as I trained to become a lawyer. And it was also contextual, so many of my family and friends would never have known what was going on.*

*I began my fascination with personal and self-development whilst I was at university (and still, annoyingly, suffering from the same condition), desperate for life to be different.*

*That was over 30 years ago now, and I am finally in a place where I truly like myself all of the time. I have trust and confidence in my gifts, and what I now know and fully accept I can do to help empower other people.*

*Yet I have never taken a single antidepressant or other drug along the way. I was always determined that it was possible to heal from within, and to find a way of effecting your own recovery. What was lacking, were the tools and resources to get the shift in thinking and perspective that could deliver the breakthrough.*

*I now know that no matter what gets thrown at me, it can't penetrate my robust core. It doesn't matter what anyone else (including my internal critic) says or does in my life, I know that I am still OK. All of the time.*

*Finally, as I turn 50, I believe it on the inside.*

All my knowledge, wisdom, insights and life experiences have pulled me like a beacon towards creating the Spirit Level Success™ System – Six Secrets of Self-Esteem (www.spiritlevelsuccess.com).

It has taken *me* a lifetime in its creation. I don't want you to waste one more minute of yours. Life is short and very, very precious.

It is my life purpose and passion to show you how you too can feel good about yourself – all the time, no matter what. Not from a place of ego, but from a serene sense of humility and caring for yourself – as though you are someone who matters. Because you do.

## So how did this all come about?

*Turn the clock back to February 2016, and I find myself sitting in a meeting room in South Africa receiving some business and personal development training. From the start of the week, we've been asked to succinctly convey our 'professional identity' and, whilst I've been self-employed for 11 years in the field of self-empowerment by this time, I just can't find the right words. I know I make a difference in my work but I'm struggling to articulate exactly what happens when I work with clients, or what the unique process is.*

*Finally, on the 5th day, the penny drops and the words 'Spirit Level Success' come to me, reflecting the gentle transformation, and the layered and organic way in which I facilitate change with my clients. The idea of a spirit level to reflect the gentle re-balancing immediately appeals to me, as it reminds me of the first thing we do whenever we take a family trip in our beloved motorhome – we check if we are level, and if not, we make some gentle, incremental adjustments until we are. I felt that this name beautifully encompassed the process, which is all about moving you towards whatever success you are seeking.*

*There was also the play on words with using the word 'spirit' – spirit level to represent the re-balancing, and also Spirit to represent higher consciousness and aspirations.*

*The final piece of the puzzle which led to the creation of the programme was that, much like myself for many years, often my clients presented as very successful to the outside world, yet secretly and to themselves, they were battling low spirit and low self-esteem on the inside, and were overwhelmed at times with self-doubt.*

And so was born the Spirit Level Success™ System – Six Secrets of Self-Esteem (www.spiritlevelsuccess.com) – working in gentle transformation for women, and men, with high success on the outside and low spirit on the inside. A simple, effective, repeatable and sustainable system guaranteed to reduce anxiety and re-balance your self-esteem and sense of self-worth – any time, every time.

Secret #1 – **Self** – where you Climb your S.T.A.I.R.™ of Self-Confidence – gets you there.

**Secrets #2 – #6** – keep you there.

Wherever 'there' is for you.

**I am a normal woman with normal everyday challenges, circumstances and emotions.** And I know that there are times when my mood dips, when my self-esteem wavers. Times when my negative, critical, unrelenting, vicious internal voice is cruel and unkind on a consistent basis.

In earlier years, I have had times when my self-esteem has dipped very low. And in the past, I didn't know what to do about it. So I had what used to feel like an agonising mountain to climb to bring myself back. In more recent years, I have taken a different approach. I have been able to step outside of my inner turmoil to have a different relationship with it, and ask myself 'what do I need to turn things around?'

All the insights and wisdom I gained from finding a way through have been invested into the Spirit

Level Success™ System – Six Secrets of Self-Esteem.

And I now know that following the strategies in this book will give me an absolute, ultimate, guaranteed way of bringing myself back to balance. Any time I need it.

*And it will do the same for you too. Guaranteed.*

There's a saying that 'sometimes you fall down because there is something down there you are meant to see'. And I believe that this is what I was meant to see, so I could help you.

Imagine how incredible and uplifting it would feel to always be able to take back the reins of your thought processes, your self-esteem and sense of self-worth because you always had available to you a step-by-step, easy-to-remember strategy for re-balancing yourself.

What you tell yourself when you're not in balance and feeling abundant is just a story. And as a story, you can decide to turn over the page and write a difference chapter to bring you back to balance and completion and a true sense of 'self' and achievement.

I have walked through that door many times in my adult life and this is the first time I have understood it all fully, and found the way to reliably and quickly turn things around. I have been a student of understanding what makes people tick and have been interested in self-help and personal development for over 30 years. Finally, I have found what I believe is the magic key, the golden thread that pulls through everything irrespective of who you are and what you do.

When I have a wobble or feel 'less than', I Climb my S.T.A.I.R.™ of Self-Confidence. You can learn how to do this and feel the instant benefits too. It will allow you to bring yourself back to a calm and centred true sense of who you are whenever you need it.

Because without an abundant and loving and caring relationship with yourself, you're missing an essential aspect of being alive.

The most important relationship you will ever have is with yourself. Why? Because how you treat yourself will either enrich or contaminate every other relationship you have in your life. When you can genuinely love yourself unconditionally, with beauty and abundance, you can be truly alive. And in that moment, you have the gift of deep connection with everyone else in your life. You really can't show anyone else true compassion if you cannot demonstrate it with yourself.

It is my dream, my motivation and my purpose to serve as many people as possible through the creation and development of the Spirit Level Success™ System – Six Secrets of Self-Esteem.

My intention is that it pulls you back from the brink and prevents you from falling over the edge into anxiety or depression. If I can help just one person avoid the need for antidepressant drugs or prevent them from developing mental health issues, then my journey will all have been worth it.

> **This book is full of techniques and strategies for regaining your sense of self, and for rebuilding your relationship with yourself from an internal position of empowerment and strength, without the need for drugs.**

I believe that when you Climb your S.T.A.I.R.™ of Self-Confidence and use the tools contained in this book, you will give yourself the absolute best and most empowering way to reduce anxiety and re-balance your self-esteem and sense of self-worth anytime, every time.

**Today, right now, is when your new story begins.**

*"Once upon a time, you grew so tired of being stuck, that you stretched yourself; pushed your way into the light and trusted you would be taken care of.........do it again."*

Liv Lane

Climb your

S.T.A.I.R.™ of Self-Confidence

**S**elf-Compassion

**T**ime

**A**ppreciation

**I**ntention

**R**aise your energy

# CHAPTER THREE

## The Spirit Level Success™ System

As human beings, we are emotional, intuitive and sensitive creatures. Historically, it was accepted that women were hardwired biologically to 'nurture and cherish', and men were more hardwired to 'provide and protect'.

Yet we all have the capacity to care so much that we take on everyone else's 'stuff' in such a way that it affects our own health and well-being. Do you have a tendency to do that?

It is often the strongest ones amongst us, the ones who put the needs of others first and who are always there for the people around them and who never ask for help, who are often the ones that suffer most greatly in their mental and emotional well-being. For boys and men, there is the added pressure of possibly having been conditioned throughout childhood not to show anything perceived as a 'weakness'.

When you try to fix everybody else, and consistently put your own needs to the end of the line, it is only a matter of time before the cracks will begin to appear and your own health and well-being will start to suffer.

Do you play many different roles in your life? Have you ever taken a moment to think about what those roles might be?

Are you the one who tries to solve everybody else's problems? Within work or family, are you the peacekeeper? the arbitrator? the wise one? the facilitator? Do you feel the need to know what's going on with everybody else so you can be the one to keep the ship afloat?

**And do you almost always put everyone else's needs above your own?**

You might find that sometimes you have 'wobbles'. That goes with the territory of being human, with all the responsibilities, expectations and challenges life throws at you whatever stage of life you have reached, and you are certainly not alone in having these. You know the kind of days when your internal dialogue is appalling and cruel, with no compassion; no filter; no limits; no off-button. An unrelenting barrage of criticism, reproach and condemnation, that swiftly and efficiently helps you sink down to the depths of despair to a place where it can feel like you have nose-dived into an abyss of complete loss of any sense of 'self'. Not only do you feel like a really bad person, you actually believe this to be true too (even though it's not).

Have you ever had days or moments like this? If you have, you'll know that it doesn't feel good.

Your brain will always filter for what you focus on. It searches for evidence that supports your point of focus, and will find similar experiences to make a connection with all that is familiar. So, already feeling like you've been knocked off your feet mentally and emotionally from your inside enemy, within a very short space of time you can feel this escalate to an almost complete loss of perspective and optimism. What this can mean is that waking up one day feeling 'a little bit down' and needing some TLC (tender loving care) can very quickly escalate into becoming a very dark place where you feel ashamed (for no discernible or rational reason), and where you find all those deep buried experiences from the past that just pour oil on the fire of how awful you are as a human being (which by the way is completely untrue, it's just that you happen to have lost your perspective in that moment).

This book sets out to help and support anyone who has a wobble from time to time. Anyone who experiences dips in self-esteem and sense of self-worth, such that it prevents you living your life in the most meaningful and fulfilling way, as life is meant to be lived. It provides a step-by-step guide to help you Climb your S.T.A.I.R.™ of Self-Confidence which will guarantee the internal shift you need to re-balance and reconnect with how special, unique and valued you are, and how deserving you are of living a wonderful life.

**It is a very different world we live in today** compared to when I was growing up in the 1970s, which was a much slower, quieter, grounded childhood than many children now experience.

In 2018 as I write, we are bombarded with a massive amount of information on a daily basis in newsfeeds, social media, emails, text messages, online advertising and so much more. In 2011 the University of Southern California carried out a study that claimed even then, that we were bombarded with the equivalent of 174 newspapers' worth of data and information every single day – five times the amount of information we received per day in 1986.

Social media is a fantastic tool in the right context, and is responsible for the success of millions of global, online businesses. And it keeps families and friends connected and present in each other's lives across the miles in a way that just wasn't possible even 20 years ago. It does though have its downside. So many people use social media as a substitute for true living, being able to hide behind the mask of a virtual identity and an online presence that is often either slightly embellished or simply not true at all. It has never been more important to be able to protect yourself from overwhelm, fatigue and the ill effects of an excess of social media in your life since, ironically, this can actually be a key contributor to experiencing low self-esteem and sense of self-worth.

Millions of people engage in Facebook, Twitter, Instagram and the like. Many people today, sometimes without realising, feel a pressure to have an online presence and to be shouting about every aspect of life as it happens. Or they spend much of their time online making subconscious comparisons between themselves and those who seemingly live a 'perfect life'. Either way, this perceived pressure to perform or the inherent, instinctive tendency to compare can have a real impact on how you feel about yourself.

> Are you living your life online, possibly missing out on the most important aspect of being alive, which is about human connection? Real connection. Being close enough to that other person that you can really see them.

If you are, please know that it doesn't have to be that way.

As you read this book and Climb your S.T.A.I.R.™ of Self-Confidence you will find a detailed explanation of each step of the process, together with a brief summary at the end of each chapter for when you need to access the information quickly. You are encouraged to read through this book in full, then learn and practise each step, so you can Climb your S.T.A.I.R.™ of Self-Confidence whenever you need it. As the saying goes, dig your 'well' before you run dry. So practise when everything is OK so the steps become automatic and 'in the muscle'. Don't wait until you feel desperate.

You can use the techniques within these pages at any point through the day or night and once you have learned to Climb your S.T.A.I.R.™ of Self-Confidence, you will have everything you need so you really will be able to make a difference wherever you are and in whatever circumstances.

Although you can dip in and out of the incredibly powerful and effective techniques contained in this book, working through the steps in order will always bring about the most effective incremental benefits. Whether you take 5 minutes or 50 minutes, you are guaranteed to get the shift you need and such will be the positive impact, you might even consider setting your alarm 5 minutes earlier so you can Climb your S.T.A.I.R.™ of Self-Confidence before you even start your day.

The Spirit Level Success™ System – Six Secrets of Self-Esteem was created to empower you to be able to re-balance your spirit level and take back control at any time – through conscious, deliberate action and thought processes, so you can proactively lift that veil of pain, despair, or discomfort.

You are invited to immerse yourself in the words of these pages long enough to change your internal state. It will sometimes be a cognitive, thinking process such as when you are invited to use your own powers of imagination or visualisation, and it will always be a real, deep, felt experience that you are invited to connect with.

The Spirit Level Success™ System – Six Secrets of Self-Esteem (www.spiritlevelsuccess.com)

is about long term, sustainable change. It is not a quick fix, although you will feel the benefits quickly. It needs to be practised and learned so you get it 'in the muscle' and it becomes an automatic lifeline you can throw yourself whenever you need it.

It is based on the wisdom collected over a lifetime of proactive learning, reflection and curiosity about what makes us tick, how we interact as human beings, how we internalise our experiences and how we can choose to live on purpose so we can live the most fulfilling and meaningful life possible.

> **This book will help you tackle low level anxiety, and challenge the status of it being normal. It's not. And there is something you can do to take back control of your life.**

When you re-balance your self-esteem so you feel better about yourself, it acts as protection against anxiety and fear. When you follow the Spirit Level Success™ System – Six Secrets of Self-Esteem it is guaranteed to bring you back to balance, so you can have the best relationship with your 'self' that is possible.

Every single trait you have is a **G.I.F.T.**™[2], without which you would not have had your experiences in the way you did or internalised them in the way you did or developed your own unique life wisdom in the way that you did.

Something has brought you to this book today. Give yourself permission to take a little time, put yourself above everything and everybody else and learn to Climb your S.T.A.I.R.™ of Self-Confidence.

In exchange, I will give you a guaranteed way of making a positive difference to how you feel about yourself and your present situation.

The Spirit Level Success™ System – Six Secrets of Self-Esteem (www.spiritlevelsuccess.com) will help you to have a different relationship with your fear or anxiety, and to place it in a different position so you can move forward in spite of it.

You will need to invest your time and energy, and do the work necessary. Not for my benefit, but for you and the life you want to be able to lead. Value yourself and your life enough to embrace everything and follow each step completely. Don't skip any parts or take any shortcuts – or it won't be as effective.

---

2. Golden Insight into Feelings and Thoughts

Much of the system is experiential, which means asking you to deeply connect within yourself and with your experience as you progress through the steps, being fully present in your body, not staying in your head simply observing your body.

At the back of this book you will find some blank journal pages with space to make your own entries, in words or images, of your insights and reflections along the way.

I hope you enjoy the journey...

*"Talk to yourself like someone you love."*

Brené Brown

# CHAPTER FOUR

## S.T.A.I.R™ – Self-Compassion

The **S** in **S.T.A.I.R.™** stands for **Self-Compassion.** Self-compassion is the first step in building your solid sense of self-confidence and self-esteem. You cannot demonstrate compassion to anyone else in a meaningful and congruent way, if you cannot show yourself true compassion in those moments when your natural instinct is to hurl internal abuse and criticism for being less than perfect; (and guess what? perfection doesn't actually exist so you can let it go).

Would you speak to your friend, or partner or child in the same way you sometimes speak to yourself if you get something wrong?

If you have done so in the past, was it an effective approach? What was their response? Did it get you the result you really wanted?

Compassion in a literal interpretation means to 'feel the pain of' another person; to be able to empathise with them; to understand and embrace their experience; to be 'with them' on an energetic and emotional level; to sponsor them, in other words to give them the message with every ounce of your being that they are welcome and valued and important. You can possibly do this quite easily for other people, yet when you need it for yourself, do you often struggle?

Imagine if you saw a small child or an elderly person, who you could see was trying their best, but needed some help or support in some way. I'm guessing that you would not hesitate to treat them with real kindness, and care – crouching down to talk to the child at their level – speaking softly and gently, in an appropriate tone of voice and pace. You probably would not hesitate to approach them from a 'nurturing' perspective.

How does this approach differ from how you speak to yourself when *you* need some help?

You can't take someone through a door you haven't walked through yourself. When you can show yourself deep, honest and true compassion; then you can do the same for other people. And when you do so, the benefits just become exponential. When you approach any situation and the people involved from a place of love and compassion, then everything changes.

62

The next time you feel angry with someone you care about, instead of staying angry, just try it on for size to see what it's like to look at them instead through the unconditional filter of love, honestly letting go of all your anger. Notice what changes.

I would like to share with you what I believe is the most powerful affirmation in the world. This affirmation brings everything you need to have a solid self-belief, self-worth and self-esteem. It doesn't presuppose that any one emotional state is preferable to another. You might not strive or wish to be happy right now, or it may not be appropriate; and yet you can still have a solid, robust core. It might be completely appropriate in your current circumstances for you to feel sad or angry; and again, you can still have a solid, robust core . And this affirmation doesn't presuppose that you have qualities or skills that are superhuman, or that you can instantaneously become something you're not just by repeating a few words.

It encourages you to engage and connect with who you really are as a human being when everything else is stripped away. To connect with and take ownership of you, in all your wonderfulness, glory and uniqueness, embracing everything about who you are.

Take a moment to read through this affirmation. Then read it again:

**I am *loveable* and *capable***
**I am *whole*, I am *unique***
**I am *strong*, I am *resourceful***
**I *matter*. I am *enough*.**

How long did that take you to read?

Did you just skim over it because you're in a rush to read on?

If you cover it over with your hand right now without looking at it again, can you recall any of the words you have just read?

Did you really connect with and feel the words?

Read it again, for a third time; and this time very slowly, v....e....r....y s...l...o...w...l...y; literally letting each word really land with you; wear it, embrace it, let it sink in – connect with each word on the deepest level possible;

**I**

**am**

**lovable**

**and**

**capable**

**I**

**am**

**whole**

**I**

**am**

**unique**

**I**

**am**

**strong**

**I**

**am**

**resourceful**

**I**

**matter.**

**I**

**am**

**enough.**

You always have been.

What was that experience like for you? What did you notice?

The real key to success when you Climb your S.T.A.I.R.™ of Self-Confidence is to *feel* the words deeply. Let them really land in your body, in your heart, in your psyche. Read them as though they are true – even if you won't quite believe it yet (and that's OK, give it time). It's important to really allow the words to resonate with you, to such an extent that you feel a shift (however small), in your energy. You must do more than just say the words. You need to *experience* them too; enough to change your internal state and emotions because only then will you really be able to make the difference you so want.

Love yourself enough to take time to go through this process slowly, carefully, and repeatedly – particularly when you have times where you can feel your sense of 'self' starting to dip. Or, when you notice that nagging ache of anxiety starting to rear its head and your sense of self-worth starting to diminish in response.

Have a strong enough desire for things to change, and the open-mindedness to give this a chance of working for you. Are you willing to do that?

Then make a decision to learn the words. Take a few moments to write out this affirmation and place it somewhere you will see it on a daily basis. Maybe on the fridge or on the inside of your bathroom cabinet door? Somewhere you know you will see it regularly every day. Repeat it several times, and repeat it often, until you know it by heart. Because knowing this affirmation by heart is the key starting point to achieving success with the Spirit Level Success™ System – Six Secrets of Self-Esteem (www.spiritlevelsuccess.com).

It's worth saying a few words here about affirmations; what they are and how you need to deal with them in order to have the greatest impact. An affirmation is a personal statement made about you which is positive and empowering, and said in the present tense *as though it is already true*. Anyone can *read* an affirmation. But simply reading or saying an affirmation out loud just isn't enough, because the danger is that you stay in a very cognitive place in your head just repeating and hearing the words. Success in their use and application will still be achieved, but it will be limited if this is all you do with any affirmation.

What you have to do instead, is to properly *experience* an affirmation. It is essential that you find a quiet space (or master the art of mindfulness so you can create your own quiet space any time wherever you are) which will allow you to have a real, felt experience of the words you are using, and which allows you to connect on a cellular level with the words, and the message behind them.

An affirmation will often be a statement that isn't technically true, but which is something that you wish to become, so it's a state or outcome you wish to bring about. For instance, if you were going for an audition or taking an exam you might be feeling nervous (if these examples don't apply to you, identify another example that is relevant to your own circumstances). If your primary focus in the lead-up to the 'event' was your fear and your nerves, it would be reasonable to expect that things wouldn't go to plan on the day. You really do get what you focus on. So with an affirmation, instead of focusing on your nerves, you would say something to yourself like 'I am confident and capable and I pass my auditions and exams with ease'.

Even though it might feel like that statement isn't completely true right now (as there may be some skills development you need to engage in, and you may have some work to do on managing your fear) – it doesn't have to be true and you don't have to *believe* what you are saying for it to make a difference and have a positive impact psychologically and physiologically.

The words you use with yourself in your internal dialogue are the crucial determining factor   with how you live your life and how successful you are – with *any* measure of success, not just in material or status terms. Those internal words that roll so effortlessly off the tongue can, and always will, have the most profound impact on how you feel. And this in turn will determine your behaviour, which leads to your results.

To understand just how powerful your imagination is, just take a moment right now to think about a type of food that you really love and enjoy. The ones that spring to mind that many people enjoy, and that often form the basis of emotional eating, are chocolate or bacon or cheese. Imagine, that next to you is either a bar of your favourite chocolate, a freshly made bacon sandwich made in the way you love it or a piece of your favourite cheese (or whatever other type of food is relevant to you).

Close your eyes and, using the power of your imagination, create an image of that food in your mind right in front of you. Really notice all the detail about what it looks like, notice all the colours, the texture, the size, the way it is laid out. Now imagine picking up the food, looking at it carefully to see how delicious it looks, smelling the gorgeousness of it, bringing it to your lips, then placing a small bite in your mouth, savouring the flavours, and noticing the taste spread like a pebble creating ripples in a pond across your taste buds that revel in the deliciousness of it all. Wow, the flavours electrify your mouth as you start to chew, and then swallow, ready to take in your next bite.

If you really did engage fully with that visualisation, you will have probably experienced some kind of physiological reaction, however small, such as salivating or a tingling sensation around your jawline.

Yet if I had simply asked you to salivate on demand, you wouldn't have been able to do it because salivating is not a process you can consciously control. Such is the power of the combination of the words, the visualisation, and the felt experience. Far more powerful than simply going through the motions. And you owe it to yourself to do more with this book than simply go through the motions.

Self-compassion is all about what you think about yourself and how you treat yourself. How you speak to yourself on the inside, how you treat your body, how you respond to yourself when you get something 'wrong'.

The first step towards any kind of change is awareness, and as you start to read this book, you may have very little awareness of how you typically speak to yourself, in other words what your internal dialogue or self-talk usually says in specific circumstances (and if you're still not sure what I mean by internal dialogue, it's that little voice that keeps saying 'what on earth is she talking about !?').

So, let me ask you about your body. How do you feel about it? Do you love every part of you? Really? Literally every part of you? Do you treat your body well? Do you nourish it with healthy food and drink choices? What kind of things do you give your body for a treat? Relaxing massages, exercise? Or alcohol and chocolate?

What about the things you say and do? Do you have such high expectations of yourself that the slightest deviation from 'perfect' (which doesn't exist by the way) will normally result in a barrage of toxic self-criticism?

The next time you 'do something wrong' and find your inner critic speaking to you in this way, pay real attention and notice the language you use, the words and the tone.

What repeated sentences or phrases does it normally use?

Make an entry in your journal and then look carefully at those words or images.

You might possibly connect more with the feelings you have before being able to identify the actual words or thoughts being used, so if that's the case, pay close attention to the feelings you get and describe them as best you can. Connect with those feelings on a deeper level, and when you feel fully connected, work backwards to understand what exactly you said to yourself to bring about that sort of feeling at that level of intensity. This process may not come easily or naturally to you right now, but rest assured it does get easier with practice.

As an example, it may be that the last time you looked in a full-length mirror you had a sinking feeling and felt deflated, either immediately or shortly after. By staying fully connected with that feeling, you were able to work out that the first thought that popped into your head when you looked in the mirror was 'oh my word, look at the state of you' or 'I look fat in this'.

Once you are able to identify the kind of language and words that you typically (and automatically) tend to use in your internal dialogue when speaking with yourself, ask yourself one important question;

*'Would I ever speak to another person in this way, out loud and to their face?'*

I am hoping that your reply will be a resounding 'No!' because it would be too cruel and hurtful.

So my next question is, 'Why then is it OK for you to speak to yourself in this way?' and what makes it worse is that you will likely speak to yourself in this way on a regular, consistent basis; on complete autopilot, so you're not even stopping to think about it and making a genuine choice. It's just happening. And you've been doing it for so long that it just feels normal.

Well guess what? *It's not OK*. Make the decision today, right now, that you are going to stop. And instead you are going to speak to yourself only with compassion. From today you are going to practise self-compassion.

Remember the words of the most powerful affirmation in the world ever?

**I am *loveable* and *capable***
**I am *whole*, I am *unique***
**I am *strong*, I am *resourceful***
**I *matter*. I am *enough*.**

Let this be your new guide and mantra to demonstrating self-compassion. As you read through the following chapters which delve more deeply into each of those qualities, you will start to take on board a different, more powerful perspective.

It may not happen straight away, after all you have probably been in a habit of relentless self-criticism for some time, so speaking to yourself through a filter of love and compassion is a new habit for you to learn. But the good news is, it's entirely possible.

**Let's begin your journey towards self-compassion.**

Close your eyes and recall as clearly as you can your earliest image of yourself at as young an age as possible. If you do have a photograph, go and find it so you have it with you.

Look at yourself in that image. How old are you? 2? 3? 4? 5?

Connect emotionally with the 'you' in that image. He or she is still a part of you today – whatever age you are. He or she still influences how you feel and behave at times. Look closely into the eyes of that young child – what do they need to experience from the other people around them, all of the time?

Yes, healthy boundaries; yes, structure; yes, freedom – but MOST importantly, above all else, that child needs to receive and know *unconditional love*. He or she needs to know that they are *loved and cherished no matter what*.

Look at yourself again in that picture and send your younger self all of the love you needed to feel back then. Look yourself in the eye and send him or her all your love right now. From your 'present self' to your 'former self'. Keep sending it back more and more intensely until the younger you really takes it on board and feels the full weight of how much they are absolutely cherished, unconditionally.

If ever you find yourself in some kind of discord with another person, it's really important to remember that, more often than not, it's about them not you.

Can you recall the last time someone made a comment towards you that you found hurtful or uncomfortable?

Whatever someone else says or does is *their* reality. They don't have the same specific information, or perspective, to see things exactly as you do. They only have their own perspective of a situation. They are entitled to their own perspective and their opinion; and you don't have to let that contaminate your sense of self. You don't have to let it infiltrate your protective energy space. You can choose to just let it go. It's not the law. It is just their view, which *just happens to be* where they are at today. They could be having a really bad day too. They could be feeling really bad about themselves and the comment they made was just a reflection of that. They could have been given misinformation. They may not have the same level of awareness as you do and would be mortified to realise that their comment had been taken in this way.

If you truly want to demonstrate self-compassion, then instead of judging yourself externally with high standards of perfection as you might from a hypothetical, parent-type figure; move to an internal place so you are *with* yourself, so that you can give compassion its true meaning and 'feel the pain of yourself'. Compassion is about being with someone in *their* world. Not collapsing into it, but still retaining your ability to have objectivity and stay emotionally safe, and to be with yourself in the way you would be with your best friend if they were in pain and suffering and really struggling.

When you're *with* yourself and have no judgment, when you treat yourself with kindness and care and recognise you have limited resources at the moment, and see that you're digging deep and using whatever you can to do whatever you need to do, that is something magical, special and amazing. Sometimes you will need to be reflective on things that have happened – that's where growth can happen – *and* you can still reflect through the lens of love and compassion, and have a solid sense of self-worth and self-esteem even though you are experiencing different and possibly difficult emotions.

In the next few chapters, we're going to explore each of the elements of this affirmation in more detail, so you have a really clearing grounding of where to place your attention when you are doing this for yourself.

# 'Self-Compassion'
# Quick Summary

Always remember that, no matter what;

I am *loveable* and *capable*

I am *whole*, I am *unique*

I am *strong*, I am *resourceful*

I *matter*. I am *enough*.

*"Sometimes you can't see yourself
clearly until you see yourself through
the eyes of others."*

Ellen DeGeneres

# CHAPTER FOUR

## Part One

### Self-Compassion Affirmation

## 'I am Loveable'

Over the years, life experiences have taken their toll. If only you could only hold on to all of the good stuff; the memories and the experiences; the perceptions; and let go of the times where you made meanings out of things that shouldn't have been made, or interpreted a comment or an incident in such a way that you felt shame or a sense of disapproval, when really there was none to be had. Your brain is very clever at storing and retrieving information, and it is very clever at filtering for information.

As a human being, you will naturally delete, distort and generalise information. Everyone does it even if you think you don't, because it's a subconscious process. And when you do this to yourself, depending on your state of mind, it can often lead to a very disproportionate sense of your own reality. If you're thinking something 'bad' about yourself, you will almost unquestionably be able to remember lots and lots of times when you felt the same way and gave yourself a hard time for something you did or didn't do; did or didn't say. And the reason why this trick of the brain can cause so much damage is that much of this activity takes place outside of your awareness, in your subconscious, so that you'll know you feel uncomfortable and have a clear sense of that, yet you're not quite sure why.

Find somewhere quiet and calm to sit down, where you won't be disturbed. Switch off or remove any distractions and settle yourself into relaxing, and calming your breathing.

Now think of someone who you have been or still are closely connected to in your life (they may or may not still be with you physically), and they adore you and cherish you. They really, really care about you, and love you deeply, *no matter what*. It might be a partner, sibling, relation, friend, child, parent, neighbour, work colleague, or anyone who is close to you; and their feelings for you are absolutely unconditional. It's OK if it takes a little time to think of the person – they are there in your life though and when you believe it, you'll see them.

Imagine now that you are sitting with this person on a sofa in a lovely, safe room, and picture as much detail as you can about the room. What size is it? What other furniture is there? What colours can you see? What is the décor like? Is the window open? Can you feel a gentle breeze coming through? Is there sunshine spilling into the room? What noises can you hear from the garden outside? Maybe some birds or the gentle hum of distant traffic?

As you sit with this person on the sofa, your bodies are turned slightly inward towards each other as though you are having a conversation. You are smiling at each other and gently holding eye contact, and as you smile at that person, you really engage with how you feel about them. What are the things about *them* that you adore? Whoever they are, there will be aspects of their personality that you absolutely love and adore. Things *you* truly love and cherish about *them*, unconditionally, no matter what.

What are the values they hold, evidenced in what they say or do, that you admire and which pull you to want to cherish and nurture them even more?

What exactly is it about that person that draws you towards wanting to be in their company, to spend your precious time with them?

How do you feel when you are with them?

Take yourself back to the last time you were with them. Go back into that memory and fully recall the whole experience. What did you feel at the time? What images come to mind when you remember that occasion? What kinds of words were being spoken? What did you feel like in your body? What emotions did you experience? And how was your breathing?

You possibly recalled all those details quite clearly and with a real sense of fondness for that person.

Yet despite all this, there will almost certainly be things that they do that you're less than enamoured of, that possibly irritate you, but because you love this person so much in light of who they are and what they stand for, you just effortlessly delete all that stuff and it seems to have no impact on your relationship. And you love them no matter what because, whether you recognise it consciously or not, you are subconsciously making a distinction at a 'behavioural' and 'identity' level. In other words, you are recognising that even though they may sometimes *behave* (through words or actions) in a way that you would prefer them not to, you realise they are human, they are learning and you recognise that part of this process we call living, is about making 'mistakes' (and hopefully learning from them).

You are also recognising, at some level, that they are *doing the best they can with the resources they currently have available.*

You are *differentiating between what they do, and who they are* – which is a vital distinction when it comes to demonstrating true compassion. Consider this carefully in relation to this specific person – does this make sense when you really think about it?

So would you then agree that if it's true for that person that they are *doing the best they can with the resources they currently have available* and that it's both possible and preferable to differentiate between *what they do, and who they are,* surely you can treat yourself with the same level of compassion and empathy when you make a mistake, can't you? I think I might already know the answer to that question. I'm guessing that, more often than not, when you make a 'mistake' or get something 'wrong' possibly the last thing you would normally show yourself is compassion. There are no mistakes by the way, there's just living and learning.

Now what I'd like you to do, is to go back in your imagination to your image of the room with this person you are sitting with and reconnect with the warm, pleasant image of you both sitting next to each other, turned slightly inwards and smiling. As you do so, imagine yourself standing up and moving into position where the other person is sitting, and stepping into their space, *as though you are them* so that you can look at yourself through the eyes of this other person. You can actually experience what it's like to look at yourself, through their eyes exactly as it would be if you were them. Now sit where they are sitting, and see yourself through their loving eyes and experiences, through their unconditional filter of love for you.

What do you see?

As you start to do this, really pay attention to everything about yourself that you notice, as though you are that person, feeling all the love, compassion and connection with you that they feel.

Now be really honest with yourself and identify all the really great things about you that they see. What are the traits and characteristics that they absolutely love and cherish about you? What little things do you do or say that they find so endearing? How would they describe you to another person? What would they say to you if they were able to speak freely? What magical words would they use? Just feel the intensity with which they adore you, unconditionally just for being who you are. And know that there is nothing at all you could ever do that would stop them from feeling like this about you. From loving you the way they do and from wanting to spend time with you. This really is the essence of true, unconditional love and you are the recipient of it.

Take a few moments to write down or draw in your journal what you become aware of – what are the qualities, characteristics and traits that you have in plentiful supply that *they* see, yet *you* sometimes forget or ignore?

How does it feel to be on the receiving end of such intense and unconditional love and affection?

Go deeper into this experience. Feel what they feel for you, and really see yourself through their eyes. What do they *really* love and cherish about you?

Are you clear what it means to love someone unconditionally?

Who have you loved unconditionally?

Someone who it literally doesn't matter what they say or do, you just have an overwhelming and unwavering sense of love and adoration for them? No conditions attached, which means that your love for them isn't dependent on them doing something or behaving in a certain way. It is such a special gift to receive and embrace. Yet so many of the relationships we enter into as adults are completely conditional; 'I love you so much unless you do this or don't do that, in which case...'

But everyone is capable of both giving and receiving unconditional love. You see, it is possible to receive this from the one person who will *never* let you down or desert you. You.

**Have you ever truly loved yourself unconditionally?**

If your answer is 'no', what stops you?

Would you be willing to give it a try as an experiment?

What if, for the next 24 hours, you agree to only communicate with yourself in your internal dialogue through a filter of unconditional love and compassion with no judgment, no blaming, no sarcasm, no sense of expectation, just pure, simple and unadulterated love?

Check the time right now and commit to yourself that, until the same time tomorrow, you will treat yourself with only kindness and compassion and love.

Notice how many times and how easily you go off into autopilot and criticise yourself for being less than perfect – it's OK though and completely understandable. You're just in an unhelpful habit, which you're now in the process of updating. This might take a little time and practice, but like developing any new skill, it is absolutely possible to retrain yourself to be kinder and more loving to yourself. And each time you stray off into self-criticism and gently guide yourself back to speaking to yourself with love, you will strengthen the new connections in your brain that will support your new habit.

To really appreciate the truth of being loveable, you do need to thoroughly get out of your head and into your body into a felt experience. It's important to step outside of your own current reality and get out of your own way, so you can go deep into your heart and soul and step outside of where you currently find yourself.

Reminding yourself that you are loveable is all about stepping into the place of specific named people that you have in your life that love you, cherish you, and care for you.

Remembering to see yourself from *their* eyes, from *their* place, from *their* position; imagining that you are right in front of them and they are looking at you. They are experiencing you and feeling everything about you that they feel when they are with you. Stepping into being that person and looking at yourself with their eyes, through their filters, allows you to let go of any filter of harshness, of judgment, of expectation or perfection, and focus your attention on the filter of love, compassion, kindness and belonging. They love you. They would never desert you, even if you did something you're not particularly proud of. They would be there for you. Always. No matter what. And so can you be for yourself.

So, you are completely loveable. Always. Loveable. And sometimes you might not believe that about yourself but actually you are.

If you can always remember this in times of difficulty and self-doubt, you will be another step closer towards developing a sound, robust core of self-esteem and self-worth.

# 'I am Loveable'
# Quick Summary

Step into the shoes of someone who adores you.

Stand in front of them and move position so you can see yourself through their eyes, with a filter of unquestionable, unconditional love.

See what *they* see, feel what *they* feel.

You are so loveable.

*"I can and I will.*
*Watch me."*

Unknown

# CHAPTER FOUR

## Part Two

### Self-Compassion Affirmation

## 'I am Capable'

Imagine that you have a sheet of thin, transparent plastic. This is your filter. And it's very special, because when you place your filter over the imaginary pair of glasses you wear to see the world and all your experiences, and many of your memories; your filter can make you interpret every different situation (whether past, present or future) in any way it likes.

You're possibly very familiar with the filter of 'I'm not good enough' or 'I can't do that' – in fact you might be something of an expert?

Can you remember the last time someone made a harmless comment to you and you made it mean something about you? Probably something negative about yourself or you just assumed you must have 'done something wrong'? (even though you hadn't, and that certainly wasn't their intention).

Can you remember how you felt? And how long you felt that way for? Did you change your behaviour as a result or miss out on something you really wanted to do because you didn't feel good about yourself?

Sometimes the automatic conclusions you reach about yourself, for no reason other than the fact that you are in the habit of doing so, can really end up having a huge impact on your life. And until you fully realise and appreciate that, it's likely to end up being a habit that continues well into your future. And your life is too precious not to break that pattern.

So how often do you actually look at yourself through the filter of 'achievement' or 'contribution' and say things to yourself like 'wow, look what I just achieved!' or 'what an amazing difference I just made to that person!'?

Being 'capable' isn't about just academic qualifications or promotions at work (even though these may still be relevant and important to you), but about *all* the ways in which throughout your life you have been able to do what needs to be done. To step up. To dig deep, even when all the odds were stacked against you.

Take yourself back now to think of a specific situation where things may not have gone to plan, but because you were involved, everything worked out fine.

What were the circumstances and who was involved?

What was it specifically that *you* contributed to the situation to bring about that outcome? What exactly did you say or do? What decisions did you make at the time that no-one else was either able or prepared to?

Write or draw in your journal about just 3 of your own life successes so far – these could be academic achievements, work promotions, business successes, hobbies, sporting achievements or anything where you have put your mind to something and achieved what you wanted (you can add more than 3 if any other examples spring to mind).

Pick just one of your life successes and take some time to go through it in depth, paying attention to what *exactly* you contributed and achieved. Identify what specific skills, qualities or characteristics you needed to have in order to achieve what you did. Write them all down in your journal, and keep adding to your list as you reflect on this success, so that you create a list of *all* the specific ways (however small) that you individually contributed to the success on that occasion.

It is so important to take full account of every small thing that you contributed to that situation. How else will you fully appreciate how completely capable and amazing you are unless you do?

In your own time, work your way through the other successes you have listed in the same way.

This is really important, so please care about yourself enough to spend an adequate amount of time on it.

Then make a habit of regularly acknowledging and giving yourself credit for everything you achieve in your life both as a human doing, and as a human *being* – which is the part that can sometimes get neglected.

Achievements through being a 'human doing' will be all the things you do that are the result of your behaviour, so everything you say and do. For instance, you might have passed your driving test or another exam or qualification. You might have travelled abroad, having planned and organised a really fabulous holiday.

Literally break each achievement down into its component parts to identify exactly what skills, qualities or characteristics you needed to demonstrate to make it happen. As an example, to plan and organise a holiday you needed to *research* the location, *co-ordinate* dates with diaries, *communicate effectively* to be clear on what you wanted, *work methodically*, be *decisive*, *prioritise* tasks, *organise* your packing etc. – and there are many more items that could be added to this list. Keep going until it's as full as possible. Because when your self-esteem temporarily deserts you or you feel 'less than' – it's those small acts of recognition that can keep you from falling over the edge.

Now think through your life so far and recall anything and everything you have ever achieved just by 'being' you. The kinds of things here are probably more relational or values-driven, and reflect more of who you are intrinsically as a person such as maintaining healthy and successful relationships, giving birth or becoming a parent, supporting family and friends, the way you parent. Or you may have helped facilitate some kind of positive outcome in a situation or helped to negotiate any fair compromise.

There are people all around you who look up to you and admire the way you go about achieving what you do, in the way that you do it. They may not tell you, and you may not be aware of it; but they do.

And they wouldn't do that unless they recognised you as being completely capable.

# 'I am Capable'
# Quick Summary

Whatever age you are right now,
you have already achieved so much
in your life. Either as a human-being or
human-doing. Pick one success and then
another and then another and identify
specifically what you had to do
to achieve that success.
You are so capable.

*"We do not need magic to transform our world.*

*We carry all of the power we need inside ourselves already."*

J.K. Rowling

# CHAPTER FOUR

## Part Three

**Self-Compassion Affirmation**

## 'I am Whole'

The day you were born and took your first breath, you arrived in this world as a whole, complete person.

You were born with everything you need – maybe not physically, but emotionally, psychologically, energetically  and spiritually (whatever that means for you). You were born whole and complete, and there is no part of you that is missing or has to be found or created. You are not broken or diminished in any way, whatever happens in your life. Everything you need is within you. You have all the resources you need, inside you already.

You may have skills to learn, but your skills *do not* and *must not* define you. Just because you need help or want to learn something, does not make you less than complete.

You may sometimes say or do things you're not proud of (you are human after all), but the part of you which generated that behaviour is still an important part of who you are (it just needs to learn different ways to express itself ).

Think about this for a minute – *you are 100% complete, and every single part of you contributes to making you whole.*

Take a few minutes to sit down in a quiet, peaceful place, close your eyes, feet firmly on the floor, hands open and resting on your legs then breathe deeply, and connect deeply within yourself. Repeat the following words to yourself slowly and meaningfully, for 3 minutes:

(On the in-breath) I am whole,

(On the out-breath) I am complete,

(On the in-breath) I am whole,

(On the out-breath) I am complete,

(On the in-breath) I am whole,

(On the out-breath) I am complete,

What do you notice when you embrace this with yourself, repeatedly and meaningfully?

Write or draw in your journal to record any shift you experience, however small, whether in your emotional state or anything else.

# 'I am Whole'
# Quick Summary

There is no part of you that is missing or
has to be found.
You are whole and complete.

*"The privilege of a lifetime is being who you are."*

Joseph Campbell

# CHAPTER FOUR

## Part Four

**Self-Compassion Affirmation**

## 'I am Unique'

Do you know that the chances of *you* being born, with all your unique genetic make-up, your inherent characteristics and your special way of seeing the world and being in the world, were massively stacked against you?

Do you realise that the fact of you actually being alive is literally a miracle? And I mean that in a really grounded, statistical sense as well as in a spiritual sense. When you do the calculation and factor in all the different variables that had to be present along the way – you can really get a sense of how totally unique you are. Yet it's so easy to forget this when you're embroiled in day-to-day living – going from one day to the next, sometimes on autopilot, because there is just so much going on – in the repetitive cycle of everything you need to do each day just to get by.

One of the most powerful ways to shift your perspective and lift yourself above your current situation is to just spend a few regular moments connecting deeply with the fact that you are a miracle, that you are completely unique and that there is literally no-one else who has exactly the same experiences, perspectives or wisdom to offer; or who can even come close to being the person you are.

Buddhists tell a story about the odds of you achieving this 'precious incarnation' of human life.

Imagine the surface of the Earth is completely covered by oceans. There is one blind turtle swimming in those oceans somewhere, who surfaces once every 100 years. There is one life preserver floating on those oceans, somewhere. The odds of you being alive are the same as that turtle surfacing with its' head through the life preserver. First time.

In 2011, Harvard graduate Dr Ali Binazir took this a step further and actually calculated mathematically and scientifically the actual odds of you being alive. He considered things like the probability of your biological father meeting your biological mother, the probability of them being attracted to each other and of staying together long enough to have you, the probability of the right sperm meeting the right egg, and of every one of your ancestors successfully reproducing in the long line of family before you, and so on. He calculated that the chances of *you*, and only specifically you, actually being alive are around 1 in $10^{2,685,000}$ which is a 10 with over 2 million zeros behind it – pretty much the equivalent of zero.

These statistics make it very clear that you are completely and utterly unique. And you are completely and utterly a miracle. No-one else is as special as you are, and no-one else will ever have exactly the same experiences or perspectives in life, or the same memories or exactly the same 'take' on any situation.

All of your individual life experiences so far have helped to shape who you are and how you see other people and the world.

No-one else could or will ever be able to achieve what you have done, in quite the same way as you did. You are irreplaceable. And very special. There *is* only and *will* only ever be one you.

*Read through these words again slowly from the beginning of the chapter starting from 'I am unique', and really let them land.*

*How do you feel when you read them, **really** read them and accept them as if they are 100% true? How do you feel when you allow yourself to believe them? Or if that's not completely possible, can you at least experiment with letting yourself believe they just might be true?*

As individuals, we each have our own way of being in 'flow'. You probably already know what it feels when you are in flow? When you get so lost in an activity or a task that time just flies by and before you know it, an hour or more has passed in what felt like just a few moments. And you feel energised, almost like your batteries have been recharged. A state of flow tends to happen when you are doing things that you both absolutely love, and are naturally talented and gifted at doing.

Some people appreciate and find flow in certainty, routine and the relative safety of knowing things in advance. For others, they thrive on spontaneity, change and freedom and would find constant certainty and routine stifling and overwhelming.

Neither way is 'better' or 'right'. It's simply about flow and preferences.

And whatever works for you, is what works for you. And that's totally OK.

Take the question of 'time-keeping' for example. I'm sure you know at least one person who is never late for anything, is always punctual no matter what, and seems to be effortlessly organised no matter what is going on? I might even have just described you?

And I'm also sure you will know someone who always seems to be flying out the door at the last minute, always arrives to meetings late (and possibly flustered) and always has a reason why they couldn't get there on time. This might describe you better?

The only difference between these individuals has nothing at all to do with whether one is better or more important, or more valid or efficient or intelligent than the other. Or whether one is more deserving, more talented, or more thoughtful than the other.

*It is literally just that their brains are wired differently, and as a result, they respond differently to the everyday stimuli they experience.*

In the case of the latter person, they will probably be creative thinkers who find it easy to get distracted with their own thought processes, solutions and ideas. They will be wired more for creativity and vision, and less so for timing and routine and so their natural tendency is to become very excited about new ideas and creativity, and they will find that they are more easily distracted.

In the case of the former, they will be wired to have a much stronger sense of timing and priority for sticking to plans. So they will be more in flow when they have more predictability about plans and will ensure that they not only leave enough time to be ready in time, but also will stay focused on the task at hand and be far less likely to get distracted.

Neither of these approaches is 'right' or 'wrong' – they are just different approaches, based on the natural tendencies of the individual concerned. It's just a different way of being, which is all part of the charm of your own uniqueness.

Albert Einstein once said, 'If you judge a fish by its ability to climb a tree, it will spend its whole life believing it is stupid'. The point being that fish are very clever and very talented *at doing what they need to do in the water*. They have no skill for climbing trees because they don't *need* to climb trees, therefore their brains aren't wired that way.

Always be considerate of others but never lose sight of who you are, even if others try to squash you into a box to fit their own agenda.

Never diminish yourself so that others don't feel uncomfortable with your uniqueness, creativity or individuality. Your positive reach and impact will be far greater when you stay true to the essence of who you are and stay in the truth of what makes you flow.

You see things completely differently to anyone else and you are influenced by all your unique experiences.

Just being born as a living breathing being gave you the right to exist and to *be*; just as much as anybody else.

Think about Dr Binazir's statistic again. The chances of you being alive are 1 in $10^{2,685,000}$. Wow. If you were a betting person, you would never take those odds on anything, yet you managed to be born in odds that, realistically, made the chances of you actually coming into being virtually zero.

But you're here.

You did it.

And that makes you very, very special.

Did you fully embrace that point? Or just skip over it?

Perhaps it might make more of an impact if you say it out loud, slowly and really feel the words.

I

**Am**

**Very**

**Very**

**Special**

In the words of Dr Binazir, *'Now go forth and feel and act like the miracle that you are'*.

# 'I am Unique'
# Quick Summary

The chances of you being born were 1 in $10^{2,685,000}$ which makes the fact of your existence a total miracle.

There is literally no-one else quite like you anywhere else in the world. You are completely unique and you are very, very special.

*"You never know how strong you are until being strong is the only choice you have."*

Bob Marley

# CHAPTER FOUR

## Part Five

### Self-Compassion Affirmation

## 'I am Strong'

Usually when you refer to someone as being 'strong', it's natural to think of that in a physical context. But whilst physical strength is important sometimes, there are other forms of strength which are just as important, if not more, such as emotional and psychological strength. You may have heard people talk about having 'strength of character', and that is the kind of strength that this affirmation refers to. You see, you really are so much stronger than you sometimes give yourself credit for.

You are strong.

Emotionally, spiritually, mentally, psychologically, energetically, physically, socially.

I know you may not feel strong right now. And if that's the case, please know that this feeling will pass. The more you are able to sit with your discomfort and feel it fully, the stronger you will become. Because when you sit with discomfort, face it and embrace it, you will come to realise that it has no real power over you.

I'd like you to cast your mind back to a time when had no choice but to be strong. Strong in whatever way you needed to be. It could have been in holding your silence, or saying the right words at the right time or being emotionally strong, just by being there for someone else. This was an occasion when everyone around you depended on you, and you delivered. When you had to really put someone else's needs above your own and you did what needed to be done; and really let someone else lean on you for emotional or other support. You found a way to dig deep, because you had to.

You have *definitely* had this experience in your life, even if you can't immediately recall such a situation straight away. Maybe it was supporting a friend or family member or work colleague through illness or bereavement. Maybe it was to support them through a significant life change.

I know you can find at least one time when you did this.

Who was involved and in what circumstances?

What **specifically** did you do or say that was evidence at the time of your strength of character? Were you a really good listener? Did you immediately drop what you were doing so you could be there for them? Did you give them a literal or metaphorical shoulder to cry on? Make notes or draw in your journal so you have a clear, physical record of the contribution you made at that time.

Then find another example, and go through the same process. Can you see how important it is to take ownership of the contribution you make?

You are strong, and there is evidence outside of you that confirms this, so always be proud of how strong you are.

# 'I am Strong'
# Quick Summary

Think about a situation where you made
all the difference, where you dug deep
and did what needed to be done. Where
another person depended on you fully
and completely, and you came
through for them. Remember exactly
what it was that you said, or did, and
what you contributed to the situation.
You really are so very strong.

*"Start where you are.
Use what you have.
Do what you can."*

Arthur Ashe

# *CHAPTER FOUR*

## Part Six

### Self-Compassion Affirmation

## 'I am Resourceful'

One of the phrases I developed a long time ago now which I find really powerful to tell myself in so many scenarios is this:

"I am doing the best I can with the resources I currently have available, *and my best is absolutely good enough*".

Please learn this phrase to ensure that you know it by heart and can say it word for word whenever you need it. Even if it's not specifically relevant to you right at this very moment, as the saying goes, dig your well before you get thirsty. What that means is that the best time to learn, practise and develop your skills and techniques is *before* you really need them, so that when the time comes, you already have what you need 'in the muscle'.

You may find it helpful to write it out several times in your journal or to say it out loud; perhaps write it down on sticky notes that you can place on various surfaces around your house if that helps, such as the fridge or your bathroom mirror; practise it, repeat it and know it. As with anything you are trying to learn, you might also find it useful to find some space in your journal and draw an image of what this statement means for you. You could draw a heart to represent the love and compassion you (are trying so hard to consistently) feel for yourself; you might draw a smile to represent that all is well in your world; literally any shape, symbol, colour or whatever. Words, language and logic engage the left side of your brain; images, colour and creativity engage the right side of your brain, so doing both represents a more holistic way of learning and makes the statement far more potent than it might otherwise be.

"I am doing the best I can with the resources I currently have available, and my best is absolutely good enough" recognises that you are human; and part of the human condition is acknowledging your limitations. On one level, there *is* no such thing as perfection. Yet on another level, you are absolutely perfect exactly as you are. It is human to be flawed, and it is human to make mistakes. And so long as you learn from those mistakes, then nothing is lost. There is no such thing as failure. There is only feedback and perspective.

You are special and unique. Each of us is completely different. You have many natural talents, gifts and abilities, some of which you embrace and show fully, whilst others remain hidden. For now.

You have all the resources you need.

You know this because you will have evidence in your life of times when you have had to find a solution or work something out, and you used skills and qualities that you didn't know you had. You have had times in your life when the chips were down and the odds stacked against you for the outcome you wanted, but you used your skills and judgment to find a way through anyway.

And on a daily basis, just by living your life, you are constantly engaged in the creative process (even though you may not realise it) of finding solutions, working things out and making things happen. On your own, without needing anyone else's input. So even though you may ask for help or suggestions from other people (which in itself demonstrates resourcefulness), you are perfectly capable of moving through any challenges being your own person, taking the right action and making the decision that's right for you and for anyone else involved.

You are so resourceful. Everything that you need is already there waiting; the only question is when and how you decide to tap into it.

Think about a particular challenge or problem you might be facing right now. When you keep looking at it from the same position and only see it from your own perspective, it may not be clear what other possible options there are for moving things on and clearing the way forward. But you *always* have the ability to shift your perspective and see things from another point of view, which *will* make a difference. It's just that you're probably asking yourself questions that aren't as helpful as they could be.

Just take a moment to ask yourself one of those really unhelpful questions that can trip off the tongue so easily when you're not feeling great about yourself like, 'why am I so useless?' or 'why can't I just do this? or 'what's wrong with me?'. Notice the barrage of all the evidence that your brain instantaneously sorts and brings to you to support the fact that you are indeed 'useless' or 'stupid', yet in reality you are not useless or stupid at all! It's just that you've asked an unhelpful question – because that is what it's natural to do when you aren't feeling great about yourself, and your self-esteem has taken a dip.

Instead, ask yourself a better question or make a better statement about yourself. For instance, 'Why Can't I?' becomes 'How Can I?' And instead of unhelpfully telling yourself that you are 'useless', 'stupid', 'a failure', 'not good enough' or whatever, see what happens when you proclaim that 'I am a valuable and resourceful person'.

Thinking about the specific problem or challenge you are facing, ask yourself the following questions and notice what happens:

* Is the way I am holding this information useful to me right now?

* Is the way I am seeing this situation useful to me?

* How else could I look at this problem?

* What else could this mean?

* What else could I bring to this challenge?

When you start to ask yourself a different kind of question, you get a different level of information and so you open up new and different possibilities and choices. Then everything changes.

What resources (skills, qualities, characteristics, traits or abilities) do you have that you are already aware of? For example, are you Patient? Tenacious? Gentle? Organised? Creative?

Write down at least 3 in your journal that you are aware of (you can add more if you'd like to)

– doesn't this show you how very skilled you are, and how adept you are at bringing what is needed to the table?

Now write down 3 different resources that you wished you either had, or had more of. Look at this second list carefully, and with an open mind. I'm going to invite you to consider that you *already have these resources in as much abundance as you need.*

You have to have them and have used them at some point in your life already, or you wouldn't recognise the absence of them now and know you needed them. So all you have to do now is remember that you already have what you need. It's already with you. Think about that carefully, and embrace that truth.

It is a really powerful statement to say and accept that you are resourceful. Everyone is resourceful. You may on occasion forget to remember those resources that you have available to you, but that doesn't alter the fact that you are still always resourceful. Just by virtue of living and reaching the age you have, you have needed to be able to work things out on so many different occasions, so often that you probably didn't realise you were doing it most of the time. But whenever you have really needed to step up, you've been able to do so.

Part of being resourceful is about understanding your relationship with some of the emotions you experience, and being able to relate to them differently instead of being consumed by them.

For instance, sometimes you might feel nervous about something that is coming up on the horizon such as a job interview, operation, performance of some kind or whatever it is, that is weeks and weeks away. It might be completely appropriate for you to feel a little nervous (this can be a good resource to tap into as it keeps you alert, focused and connected with the experience, and it raises your standards) but starting to feel nervous now, this far in advance, may waste a significant amount of your energy.

So you have a choice and can decide to change your relationship with it. What if you gave yourself permission to choose whether you'd like to feel nervous now or delay it by a few weeks? Thinking of it in this way changes your relationship with it when it feels like a choice, rather than an inevitability. Would that make a difference for you?

And if you do choose that you'd like to delay feeling nervous about the event or situation, then make an agreement with yourself about how far in advance of the date would be useful and appropriate.

So for instance with that job interview, you might say that 3 weeks of nerves in advance is plenty (or 5 days or 24 hours or any length of time that works for you). If you are still 8 weeks away, do everything you can to prepare but place an internal emotional boundary on your nerves. If you start to feel them ahead of time, just gently tell yourself 'no, it's not the right time yet. I may (e.g. I have permission to) feel nervous in another 5 weeks' time. Just not today'.

In effect, what you are doing is using your resourcefulness to *pause* the emotion that you know *could* have a detrimental impact on how you feel about yourself right now, knowing you can come back to it whenever you want to when it is the right time to feel that way.

It might be that the emotional state you are experiencing is one that you don't feel you *can* choose to delay, in which case you may prefer to use a different technique to change your relationship with it.

Your brain does not know the difference between what is real and what is made up. This fact is part of what can contribute to developing low self-esteem, because when you have an internal barrage of negative and highly critical statements flowing towards you like a river, it can become difficult to cope with and even more difficult to effectively shield yourself from the inevitable detrimental impact on your mental and emotional health and well-being.

Your thoughts will always determine how you feel, and your feelings influence how you behave. That's an accepted cyclical connection in psychology. So it can soon escalate into something more serious when you are running a programme in your mind that consists of constant belittling, reproach, blame and condemnation from your internal dialogue. And all based on statements that are generally, if not completely, untrue.

By the same token, you can also visualise or re-programme your brain with anything you like that is helpful and constructive and, even if it isn't strictly true, your brain will eventually accept it as true and change your physiology accordingly. This is why affirmations and visualisations are so powerful, because with repetition and deep connection they will eventually become ingrained into your subconscious *as though they are true*.

You can use this strategy as a means of helping yourself to regain and re-balance your self-esteem and sense of self-worth when you need to, in a way which is very effective.

You can also use visualisation to dissolve the energy around an emotion that you no longer wish to experience if it's not serving you.

Imagine that you were feeling really anxious or fearful, in circumstances where it wasn't helpful or it was holding you back in some way. Use your imagination to create a picture in your mind of what your fear or anxiety would look like in relation to how it feels right now. Crystallise as many details as possible that relate to your picture such as:

* Is it black and white or colour?

* Is it a solid form with clear edges? Or more abstract?

* Is it moving or still?

* Is there a sound associated with your fear or anxiety?

* Where is it positioned in relation to your body? Is it inside, if so where? Or is it outside of your body? And if so, is it in front of you? Above you? Behind you?

* Is it close up or far away?

* What other details do you notice?

Now really focus on the image in your mind's eye, and experiment with what happens to the intensity of your fear or anxiety if you focus on and adjust certain aspects of the picture, one at a time, for instance:

* If there is movement in your picture, what happens if you make it go still?

* What do you notice when you move the position of the picture? For instance, if it was in front of you and above, what happens if you move it to the side and lower down?

* What do you notice if you move it further away from you, into the distance?

* Was your picture in colour? If so, change it to black and white. If it was that already, reduce the contrast so it looks more blended and grey. What happens?

* Was there a sound associated with your picture? What do you notice if you turn the volume down gradually until it is silent?

* What happens if you step back from the picture, and disassociate from it?

* Could you move and look at it from another side or perspective? What do you notice if you do this? Does it feel smaller, less impactful from there? If not, move again to another different position.

* What's your experience when you make the sides close in and the picture reduce in size?

Remember, these questions all relate to the visual representation of what you are experiencing as an unhelpful feeling of fear or anxiety – so as you go through the questions, you are taking the action suggested then constantly checking in and referencing how these changes compare to the original intensity of the feeling. Anything that makes it feel less intense and therefore more comfortable you can choose, through your resourcefulness, to keep. Any action that makes it feel more intense, you can discard.

Once you have made your feeling as manageable as possible, you can watch it as you make it shrink smaller, smaller, smaller and smaller still. You are in control of the images in your mind so even though you might need to concentrate greatly, you can make this image do whatever you want it to.

Once it becomes so small it will fit on the tip of your finger, you have a choice of what to do with it, depending on whether it is useful for you to hold on to some of that emotion. If it is, then watch it move slowly down, down, down your body all the way into your big toe so you still have it when it's needed but it's not overwhelming you and in control. In this way, it becomes a resource you can tap into when you need it because as you already know, sometimes a little bit of fear or nerves can be a good thing, depending on the situation.

If the feeling you worked with is not one that you want to hold on to, then instead as you shrink it making it smaller, smaller, smaller, this time you see it become a speck on the tip of your finger – from where you can blow it away into the atmosphere. Pay really close attention to how all this visualisation has lessened the intensity of your original feeling. This is your resourcefulness at its absolute highest. And having done this once, you will now be able to use this strategy whenever you need to in the future.

You have the capacity to do whatever you want at any time, or to find out how.

# 'I am Resourceful'
# Quick Summary

You have all the resources you need already inside you. Remind yourself of the qualities, skills, characteristics and traits you have and recall times when you have used creativity and flexibility in your approach to find a way forward when you have faced a problem or difficulty. Be grounded in the knowledge that you can choose to have a different relationship with any emotion you experience, at any time, simply by using your imagination and skills of visualisation. You can ask for what you need and you can get what you need.

*"You cannot get through a single day without having an impact on the world around you. What you do makes a difference. And you have to decide what kind of difference you want to make."*

Jane Goodall

# CHAPTER FOUR

## Part Seven

### Self-Compassion Affirmation

## 'I Matter'

You are important.

In all circumstances, in any situation.

It doesn't matter who is involved; what role you are in or what 'hat' you are wearing. You matter. This is a fact, beyond question (even though you might forget to remember this at times).

When things start to feel a little tough or you're feeling like your self-esteem is deserting you, it's human nature to question yourself. But often in such circumstances, the kinds of questions you ask yourself can be unhelpful at best and absolutely devastating at worst.

You see, when you ask yourself a question, your brain will automatically default to finding whatever evidence and examples it can to answer your question – *literally*. So if, in the heat of the moment, you've ever asked yourself something like, 'why am I so stupid?', you probably had immediate flashbacks of all the times you'd behaved in a way that the critical part of you would have classed as 'stupid'. Your brain will literally just answer your question – it won't rationalise it and contradict you. Especially if you are in the habit of automatic self-criticism, instead of automatic self-compassion.

It is more common than you think to question yourself with the kind of challenges that start with 'Why can't I just....?', 'Why aren't I just....?', 'Why don't I just....?'.

What kind of questions do *you* typically ask yourself that demonstrate an underlying belief that you don't count, or that you're not as important as everybody else? Note these down in your journal. Take enough time to fully reflect and write down each one that comes to mind.

Now take each of those (unhelpful) questions in turn, and challenge it by changing the words around, and instead ask yourself a question that starts with more powerful and empowering words, such as 'How can I....?', 'How do I.....?', 'How will I.......?'

Try reframing each of your questions into a different question in this way; focusing on what you *can* do rather than what you can't.

What does each question become instead?

For example, 'Why can't I just stick to my diet?' could become 'How can I learn to eat healthily?' and 'Why can't I just stop drinking alcohol?' could become 'How can I learn to value my body and health more?'.

And 'Why aren't I more patient?' could become 'How can I use my desire to get things done in a positive way?'

You matter. No matter what. Your opinion counts. Your being here, counts.

So find your voice. Speak up and speak out. Do it once, and see how it gets easier.

# 'I Matter'
# Quick Summary

You have a right to be here. And you count.
You matter just as much as anyone else.
And you make a difference to the people
around you every single day.

*"You Are Enough.*
*Not because you did or said or thought*
*or bought or became or created*
*something special.*
*But because...*
*you always were."*

Liv Lane

# CHAPTER FOUR

## Part Eight

### Self-Compassion Affirmation

## 'I am Enough'

From the moment you were born and started breathing and existing independently, you were enough. You are now. You always have been. And you always will be. Your being enough is never dependent on anything else.

You don't have to *do* anything to be enough. You don't have to *learn* anything. You don't have to *behave* a certain way. You don't have to *please* anybody else. You don't have to be earning a certain amount of money, or have a particular professional title.

You really are enough. Just as you are.

Sometimes, in some circumstances, you may question whether you are enough. Or you may have developed a long held limiting belief that you're not good enough.

There is no arbitrary judge out there who has everything worked out and is the independent arbiter of whether what you do or don't do is OK or enough. This is all a construct of your ego and your irrational fear.

In some contexts, such as parenting or perhaps in your role at work, it's natural to occasionally question and second guess yourself. It does not mean you are doing anything 'wrong'. So think about the context, and then move position so you shift your perspective and see it from another position. Always ask yourself the question, what *else* could this mean?

Take a few minutes to sit down in a quiet, peaceful place where you won't be disturbed. Close your eyes, place your feet firmly on the floor, and hold your hands open and resting lightly on your thighs. Keep a firm but comfortable position in your spine, so you're consciously holding your posture in a dignified way, to avoid slouching. Then breathe deeply, and connect deeply within yourself. Repeat the following words to yourself slowly and meaningfully, for 3 minutes:

(On the in-breath) I am enough,

(On the out-breath) I am enough,

(On the in-breath) I am enough,

(On the out-breath) I am enough,

(On the in-breath) I am enough,

(On the out-breath) I am enough,

What do you notice when you say this to yourself? Note in your journal any shift you experience (however small) whether in your breathing, your emotional state or anything else.

You really are enough. You do not need any kind of external validation from anybody else. Just by virtue of living and breathing, you are enough.

In the words of the incredibly inspirational and successful Nic Vujicic who was born with no arms and no legs, 'It's a lie to think you're not good enough. It's a lie to think you're not worth anything'.

# 'I am Enough'
# Quick Summary

**'I am now and I always will be enough.'**

*"I have come to believe that caring for myself is not self-indulgent. Caring for myself is an act of survival."*

Audre Lorde

# CHAPTER FIVE

## Part One

## S.T.A.I.R™ – Time

### to Pause (to be Present)

The **T** in **S.T.A.I.R.™** stands for **Time** and, more specifically, taking the **Time to Pause**, **Breathe and Assess** your current reality.

Pausing in life is something that often gets forgotten about, or is pushed to the bottom of the pile. In fact, many people don't ever consciously think about specifically scheduling time to mentally pause, rest and take stock at all, even though they may be in the habit of physically resting when their body feels tired.

Life can be so busy these days unless you make a conscious choice to live it differently, and more mindfully. Many people just don't and so it's not surprising that levels of stress and overwhelm generally are escalating, along with the rise in engaging in unhealthy habits such as over-eating or drinking to support emotional discomfort.

The reality is that you cannot fix or change anything in your life if your head is saturated or you feel emotionally bombarded. Because in that state, there really is no room for any kind of change to happen or movement to take place.

Pause long enough to notice where you may have retreated to within yourself; have you gone so far inside that you are experiencing everything very intensely from your own viewpoint and internal perspective? This position can perpetuate ruminative and unhelpful thinking. That sense of just going round and round in circles, over and over replaying the same thoughts, circumstances and scenarios.

Come back outside and regain your perspective. Ground yourself by asking yourself questions based on paying really close attention to your senses, your surroundings, and everything you can physically see, hear and touch right now in the present moment. Speak out loud if that's appropriate and, if not, this works just as well saying it internally so long as you keep your focus. Work your way through each of your senses in turn, answering your own questions in minute detail and for as long as necessary to restore a sense of calm and balance, and regain your sense of connection to your surroundings.

For example, if you are sitting outside in your garden, to connect with your sense of sight you might ask yourself the question, 'What Can I See?' and reply by saying something like, 'I can see the green strands of grass gently blowing in the breeze, I can see a daffodil with its' pretty yellow flowers, I can see small garden birds on the tree in front of me, I can see birds gently pecking at the seeds in the holder, I can see a few seeds on the ground underneath the holder where they have fallen, I can see the wooden panels of the garden fence, I can see the blue sky and white clouds above me, I can see the fields beyond and the cows in the fields, I can see......' and so on, continuing to identify and name each specific detail that you can physically see in front of you, for however long you need to.

Then, follow the same process with your sense of hearing. So you ask yourself the question, 'What Can I Hear?' and you might reply by saying something like, 'I can hear the traffic on the road as it drives past my house, I can hear the birds tweeting as they fly around the garden, I can hear the water gently trickling from the pond, I can hear the leaves rustling on the trees and plants with the gentle breeze, I can hear the clock ticking, I can hear my family talking in the background, I can hear a neighbour mowing their lawn, I can hear the rhythmic sound of my own breathing, I can hear....' and so on, naming all the specific individual sounds you can hear. Do make sure that you listen carefully for *everything* you can hear, keeping your focus so that you identify all the sounds around you. And even when you think you have them all, listen harder, there will be more.

Then continue by focusing on your sense of touch, and ask yourself the question, 'What Can I Feel?' You might find it helpful to move towards specific items or objects as you work through this particular sense so that you can actually feel the different textures and surfaces of what is around you, and you might reply with something like, 'I can feel the weight of my body on the seat, I can feel the texture of the fabric of my clothes, I can feel the grass between my fingers, I can feel the bark of the tree and how rough it feels as it protects the goodness inside the trunk, I can feel the texture of my hair, I can feel the ring on my finger with the smoothness of the band, and the bumps of the clasps around the stone, I can feel the skin on my face....' and so on.

If it's relevant to you, you can also do this with your senses of taste and smell – it might be flowers, perfume or aftershave you can smell, and you may be drinking coffee or be able to taste your last meal or toothpaste.

If you have woken through the night and are possibly struggling to get back to sleep you can still follow this process. Instead of naming what you are *actually* seeing, hearing and feeling though, you will walk yourself through the process from your memory of the room you are in (or another familiar place if it is easier to recall the details). So if it's a bedroom in a house that you've lived in for a reasonable period of time, you will be familiar with the room and be able to walk yourself through what you can see in your imagination from memory. If you're half awake, you will probably be able to hear certain specific sounds such as the clock ticking, your partner breathing or the traffic outside. And when it comes to your sense of touch, again you will know your room well enough to be able to imagine yourself walking up to specific items or surfaces to know what they would feel like as if you were actually touching them.

So what is the point of all this? Pausing your life and reconnecting with your senses is one of the most effective ways to get grounded. To connect with yourself and your reality, and to get out of your mind (just for a little while) and into your body.

Your body is always in the present moment. It always gives you instant information and reacts to whatever is happening in the here and now. It will tell you if it's thirsty or hungry. And it will quickly respond and move away from something that is too hot or too cold. Your body knows how to react instinctively in any situation. What often gets in the way is your mind. So, for instance, your body knows when it's not hungry and is just thirsty (the physical signals you receive are the same for both), but it's your mind that gets you going for the biscuit tin instead of the glass of water; or the alcohol or the cigarette or whatever other emotional crutch you might be in the habit of using to manage your emotional ups and downs.

Going through the process of reconnecting with your senses brings you back down to reality, and can help you move away from the destructive thoughts that may be currently plaguing you.

The second step to successfully pausing to be present is to connect with your own life-force and heartbeat. Connecting with your heartbeat is a really powerful way to bring you out of your head and into your body. After all, it is your heart and your heart alone that is the reason why you are living and breathing at all right now. The miracle of that one organ in your body is so precious, so connect with it and feel it for a minute or two and see what a difference it makes. You can do this almost literally at any time, in any circumstance.

Using your index and middle fingers (not your thumb as this has its' own heartbeat), position your two fingers on one of your pulse points — the side of your neck in the hollow between your front windpipe and below your ear; to the front of the middle part of your ear directly in front of the opening, or on the inside of your wrist.

It might take you a few goes to find it if you're not used to taking your own pulse but trust me, it's there and you will find it.

When you do, you might wish to close your eyes so you can zone out of everything else other than the feeling of your heart pumping and your blood pulsing through your veins. Truly living in the moment is not a cognitive process that takes place in your head. It is a living, sensory and responsive experience.

Connect with the miracle of living right now. In the present moment. With no expectation or judgment about the moment that has just passed, or the moment ahead of you.

This is totally real. You are alive.

## 'Time to Pause (to be Present)' Quick Summary

Make a decision to stop, even for just
a few moments, to allow yourself to
become fully grounded and be
present in the moment.
Connect with each of your senses
in turn – naming out loud everything
you can see, hear and touch.
Then everything you can smell and taste
(if relevant). Then connect with your
heartbeat and stay connected long
enough to appreciate
the joy of being alive.

*"Sometimes the most important thing in a whole day is the rest we take between two deep breaths."*

Etty Hillesum

# CHAPTER FIVE

## Part Two

## S.T.A.I.R™ – Time

### to Breathe (as you Body Scan)

The next step in the process is taking **Time to Breathe**. Many people never take the time to connect with the miracle of breathing in any kind of conscious way, yet your breath is your life force and always with you wherever you are; always present, always there for you. And it is the only physiological process in your body that you have any conscious control over. So if you let it, your breath can always be your first friend to help you if you start to feel anxious or if your self-esteem might be about to desert you for a little while. Your breath will always be able to help you regain a sense of calm and balance.

You can use these techniques at any time of the day as well as through the night. Whether you are sitting, standing, walking or lying down, they will help. If you do wake in the night with your mind racing and doing all the things it likes to do, you can start by acknowledging to yourself that resting is still beneficial, so you can let go of worrying about trying to go back to sleep, and you can breathe deeply and on the in-breath and out-breath say to yourself;

Sleep (in-breath) and rest (out-breath)

Sleep (in-breath) and rest (out-breath)

Sleep (in-breath) and rest (out-breath)

By focusing on those words, and placing your attention firmly on your breathing, you can avert the risk of your brain engaging in repetitive thinking patterns that either wake you up even further through the night or get you waking too early in the morning. During the daytime, you could change the words so it becomes;

Safe (in-breath) and calm (out-breath)

Safe (in-breath) and calm (out-breath)

Safe (in-breath) and calm (out-breath)

Another powerful technique for breathing deeply and impactfully, is to imagine there is an 8-bar piece of music playing and to count and breathe in time to the music, including the half-beats, in continuous breaths something like this;

One-ah Two-ah Three-ah Four-ah

In......................................... Hold

One-ah Two-ah Three-ah Four-ah

Out..................................... Hold

One-ah Two-ah Three-ah Four-ah

In......................................... Hold

One-ah Two-ah Three-ah Four-ah

Out..................................... Hold

Always ensure when you are practising any kind of breathing technique that you breathe slowly, fully and deeply – so you completely expand your lungs on the in-breath – noticing your chest rise and your diaphragm lower and then fully empty your lungs as much as is comfortable on the out-breath, noticing your stomach rise as you exhale.

It feels really good to connect fully with your breath and to use it as a soothing aid to restful and mindful meditation.

Breathing through your nose, bring your attention to the area just below your nostrils to the point where your breath leaves and enters your body. As you focus on your breathing you might like to gently count in for 3 and out for 3 in time to the flow of your breathing, connecting with the even rhythm of your in-breath and out-breath; in-breath and out-breath; in-breath and out-breath. Nothing forced, just settling into the natural rhythm of your body.

When you feel more settled and your breathing is regular, you may release the counting and instead, just start to notice how connected you are to whatever is beneath you that you are resting on, whether you are sitting, standing or lying down. Feel connected to the chair, the floor or the bed beneath you, and notice how whatever you are sitting or lying or standing on supports you unconditionally and unquestionably, as it itself is supported unconditionally by Mother Earth, going down and down and down for miles beneath you – always ensuring that you are completely and utterly supported from below. Unquestionably and unconditionally that physical and energetic support is there for you. You cannot fall.

And as you start to feel calmer, you can complete a Body Scan, moving through each part of your body in turn starting from the top of your head, so you check in with each part, noticing anything of interest, releasing any tension and giving gratitude for your health along the way. Although you can perform a body scan anywhere, you may find it more helpful to do this in a place where you can lie down and relax and where you can avoid being disturbed.

Sometimes if you feel anxious or uncomfortable, it is natural to hold on to tension in certain parts of your body. And quite often, you may not realise you are holding on to this tension because it is something you have been so used to doing automatically for so long. If you are using this technique through the night because you are struggling to get to sleep, do pay particular attention to how you might be holding tension in your head and neck area so that you can consciously release any tension there as you learn to **M.E.L.T.™** into your bed or chair or whatever it is you are lying or sitting on:

**M**ake – consciously decide and choose to do this

**E**verything – every single cell, each individual part of your body

**L**et go of – release it fully and unconditionally

**T**ension – any tightness, stiffness, pressure or rigidity

Imagine that you are holding what looks like a large tennis racket with the strings missing, large enough to move effortlessly and freely over your whole body. When you place a part of your body through the gap where the strings used to be, it magically allows you to fully focus your attention just on that one specific part of your body, noticing what you notice and releasing any tension as you allow each part of your body to **M.E.L.T.™[3]**.

Starting at the top of your head, scan slowly downwards through your forehead, eyes, nose, ears, mouth and chin towards your neck and shoulders. As you complete your body scan, know that you are loved, and imagine bringing a bright white light of love and protection with you on your scan, that is life-affirming and energy-bringing. You might also find it comforting to repeat the words, 'I am loved and blessed' at the same time.

As you move your attention through your body, focus on each specific area long enough to be aware of anything of interest such as slight aches or pressure, and long enough to consciously release any and all tension you become aware of. Move down slowly through one shoulder, down through one arm, elbow, forearm, wrist, hand and

---

3. Make Everything Let go of Tension

each individual finger releasing tension as you go. Then gently back up to your shoulder, slowly across your shoulder blades and then down the other arm, elbow, forearm, wrist, hand and fingers before returning gently and predictably to your shoulder blades.

Then continue slowly on, down through your chest, lungs and breathing system, through your torso, belly and reproductive system, continuing down through your buttocks to the top of one leg, slowly down your thigh, knee, calf, ankle, foot and each individual toe noticing and releasing as you gently move along, then slowly back up to return to your buttocks before moving down through your other leg, slowly down your thigh, knee, calf, ankle, foot and each individual toe.

Then from here, moving slowly back up towards your buttocks, rising through your reproductive system, your belly, torso and up through your chest and breathing system, your shoulders, neck and head and beyond towards your Higher Self.

# 'Time to Breathe (as you Body Scan)' Quick Summary

Consciously become aware of your breathing
as you M.E.L.T.™[4] and complete a
gentle Body Scan noticing what you notice,
releasing all tension.

---

4. Make Everything Let go of Tension

*"There is no happiness without freedom, and freedom is not given to us by anyone; we have to cultivate it ourselves."*

Thich Nhat Hanh

# CHAPTER FIVE

## Part Three

## S.T.A.I.R™ – Time

## to Assess (the Arguments)

Next we take **Time to Assess** the 'For and Against' of what you are telling yourself on the inside.

What kind of questions do you ask yourself when the going gets tough? When you are feeling anxious or 'less than'?

As you know, your brain works in a very literal way, so if you ask yourself a question that isn't helpful or supportive, you will get an answer that you probably don't want.

You will always get more of what you focus on. It's a little like having your own in-built search engine so if you ask yourself a question like, 'Why am I such an awful, useless failure?' your brain will work on that as a filter and throw back at you every single possible fact or piece of evidence it can find to answer the specific question you have asked.

When you are feeling low, it's essential that you avoid asking yourself questions the answers to which will show you how 'inadequate, useless (or whatever other untrue, harsh words you typically use with yourself)' you are.

Ask yourself a better question, one that requires your brain to find some supportive and constructive evidence about how wonderful you are. Instead of 'why am I so (insert your own brutal word or words of choice here)?' what other question could you ask yourself that presupposes you are a special, lovable and capable human being? For instance, 'in what positive ways specifically have I connected with other people today?'

It's always useful to check where you are placing your attention. Are you problem-focused? or solution-focused? Wherever you place your attention is what you will get more of, because this focus acts as the filter through which your brain sifts for, processes and sorts information, deleting much of what isn't relevant. Where you tend to focus is just a habit. So if you start to realise that you tend to always dwell on a problem and get stuck in the detail of it, always remember that you have a choice and, at any time, you can choose to start paying attention to possible solutions instead. And you can choose at any point to metaphorically walk around to the other side of the problem and get a completely different perspective of it.

Try this simple test and you will see how easy it is for your brain to start registering what you place your attention on when it becomes your conscious point of focus.

Whether you are a car driver or not, if you are out on the roads as a driver, passenger, cyclist or pedestrian on a fairly regular basis, you will probably not consciously notice the different colours of cars as they pass you. Your brain will be in the habit of automatically deleting much of that information as it's not needed, and it has to delete most of the information it is bombarded with every day or it wouldn't be able to process it all and you wouldn't be able to cope.

Next time you go out on the roads, make a conscious decision that you are going to deliberately notice all the red cars out there. It's like setting a point on a compass and you will be surprised at how many red cars you now notice.

Then expand your field of reference to include anything at all that is red so you might start noticing things such as post boxes, front doors, berries on the trees or flowers. And again, you will be surprised at how much you notice that, previously, you hadn't even really registered. Yet all those reds things were there all along.

If you stay problem-focused, your brain will do the same thing and find as much supporting evidence and information for the problem state (eg 'no-one likes me', 'why am I such a failure?') as it can.

Assess what you are saying to yourself with the facts and evidence available and explore with curiosity.

Is what you are saying to yourself *actually* true? If so, is it actually true *100% of the time in every situation, in all circumstances?*

Take a statement like 'no-one likes me' or 'I'm a complete failure'. What would it mean if it *was* absolutely true 100% of the time, no exceptions? I'm sure you agree it would be devastating and overwhelming.

Remember that your thoughts will always dictate how you feel, and how you feel will always determine how you behave, so is it any wonder then that you feel so down if this is the programme you are running in the background? Maybe you're not sure why, but you just have a strong sense that life isn't what you expected it to be and it's not quite as much fun as you were expecting (maybe at times even feels like it's not worth living?).

Take a look at that statement again (or whatever statement you tend to use with yourself). Isn't it actually the case that this statement is *not* true all the time, *not* true in every context, and not true in relation to every single person you know?

In fact, what actual facts or evidence do you have that this statement is true in *any way at all?*

You only know what you actually know to be true for a fact if you have been told first-hand by the person who does know (not by someone speculating) or it's an unequivocal fact and the evidence is already 'out there'. Anything less than this is your brain making up a story that is not based in truth and reality, but in speculation and fantasy, fuelled by your inner critic.

You may be able to recall perhaps one occasion where maybe things didn't quite go to plan or you possibly said or did something that, on reflection, you wish you hadn't.

Sometimes words just slip out automatically, or you behave in a way you wish you hadn't. But you are not alone. Everyone has moments like this at some point, even though they may not have the self-awareness yet to realise.

You can lessen the intensity of the impact of those thoughts. Even if you feel you can't, or won't or it doesn't feel right to let them go completely (which is your choice), you can still get a different perspective on them.

So, name that one person and that one circumstance. XXXX told me they thought I was YYYY on that day when I did or said ZZZZ.

And then question yourself – do you know for a *fact* that this is what they thought? Or are you mind-reading? Are you making up a story? If you are, then there is no way you could possibly *know* for a fact what they were thinking. Is there? It's just as likely that they were thinking something kind and compassionate about you as not. Isn't it?

The statement you keep repeating to yourself and playing in the background, far from being 100% true all the time in every context, may not be true at all, ever, in any context. Even if you believe it is true, this was a one-off situation when your personal standards fell short for less than a minute. What proportion of your life would that minute represent? (Take that minute as a percentage of how many minutes you have been alive so far – it's such a small percentage as to be almost negligible).

We all have life experiences that, with hindsight, we'd change. Things we said, things we did. Maybe in drink, maybe not.

These experiences don't define you. Let them go.

When you are at your lowest points you possibly replay them, but the other people involved won't be doing so.

It's a form of self-induced torture. You have nothing to be ashamed of. You did, said or behaved in whatever way you did, said or behaved at the time. For better or worse. You cannot turn back time or 'un-spill the milk'.

If there is reparation to perform, do it now. Make amends. Write that note. Say you're sorry – if you can and if it's appropriate.

Or let it go now.

If you can't rectify because the person has left, moved away or died, then take a quiet moment to say to them out loud what you would have said to them in person, and with a gentle prayer let those words float off into the atmosphere and let the whole scenario go along with it.

Draw the line underneath, and allow yourself the closure you so badly need.

Will this matter to you this time next year? Will it matter to you in 5 years' time? Quite possibly not.

What would you tell your best friend if they were replaying old experiences in this way and it was having such a detrimental impact on them? And what would your best friend say to you if they knew you were suffering in this way?

You are always at a point of choice. And you can always choose to change the language you use with yourself on the inside.

# 'Time to Assess (the Arguments)' Quick Summary

**Check out the arguments for and against what you are saying to yourself:**

* Can you ask yourself a better question?
* Are you problem-focused or solution-focused?
* Is what you are saying to yourself 100% true, all of the time?
* How will you feel about this 5 years from now?
* What would your best friend say to you?
* What would you say if it was your best friend saying this to you?

*"As we express our gratitude, we must never forget that the highest appreciation is not to utter words, but to live by them."*

John F. Kennedy

# CHAPTER SIX

## S.T.A.I.R™ – Appreciation

The **A** in **S.T.A.I.R.™** stands for **Appreciation**. Appreciation and gratitude are qualities that are so important to maintaining a healthy sense of self. When you are grateful for everything you have in your life, both material and non-physical, you give yourself an amazing opportunity to immediately improve your mood and to improve how you feel about yourself. This is because when you give thanks, you always receive.

Appreciation is about living in the moment and slowing down long enough to really enjoy what you have around you, so you can notice every little detail and take joy from the little things in life.

Do you need to learn the art of not rushing to finish one thing just so you can quickly start the next?

Do you need to slow down long enough to remember that life really is a journey and not a destination?

In the words of John Lennon, 'Life is what happens while you're busy making other plans' – so why not enjoy every single moment consciously, give thanks and appreciate all that you are surrounded by.

There's an old adage that says if you continue rushing head-long through your life, there will come a time when the Universe will whisper to you to slow down and enjoy life. Obviously there won't be an audible whisper, but something might happen that will give you a bit of a hint that maybe you could benefit from taking things a little more slowly and appreciating your life more. If you don't listen the first time, the Universe will speak to you more firmly and invite you again to slow down and enjoy the process of your life. This might be represented by a more significant event that happens to you.

And then if you still won't listen, it will metaphorically bang you over the head to *make you stop* and appreciate your life. You may know of people who have had a major health scare which changed their life and their outlook significantly. Such an event can be life-affirming for the person concerned and it often acts as a catalyst to look at life differently and appreciate everything, so now they make time to 'stop and smell the roses'.

You have an opportunity to introduce appreciation into your daily routine and experience the uplifting benefits of being grateful for everything.

There are four areas that you can consider to help you really appreciate everything you **H.A.V.E.™** in your life:

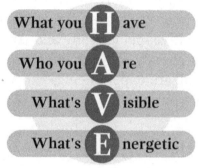

What you **H**ave

Who you **A**re

What's **V**isible

What's **E**nergetic

Appreciation, as with each step you take when you Climb your S.T.A.I.R.™ of Self-Confidence is not just a thought, or a quick cognitive process. It is a deeply felt experience that you may need to practise on a daily basis so you feel the real benefits and become something of an expert.

Sometimes if things aren't quite going your way or maybe finances are a little tight, it can be easy to focus on what you *don't* have, and feel a sense of lack or neediness. It can be very easy to stop noticing all the good things that you do still have going on in your life and all the good things that you could still appreciate.

Holding the energy of lack or neediness will almost always be counter-productive because the Universal Law of Attraction holds that you will attract towards you exactly what you put out, just like a magnet or a boomerang that returns to where it started. If you aren't even able to appreciate what you already have, why would the Universe bring you more of it? It makes sense if you think about it. So even though it might feel counter-intuitive, being really and truly grateful for what is already in your life in spite of any adversity you are experiencing, will always reap rewards for you.

## What you Have

When you think about everything you have materially in your life, would you normally take the time to give thanks for it? Or do you tend to hold more of a sense of entitlement and take your possessions for granted a little?

Showing appreciation of what you have for whatever length of time you will have it for, will shift the energy around you in a really positive way.

You see, you never *really* own anything. It's all transient. And you really can't take anything with you when you leave, the same as you didn't bring anything with you when you were born. When you leave, it will literally be just you and your body.

It's really important to appreciate every single thing that you have, however you came about it. And that doesn't mean you can never let things go. Sometimes it's the right time to let an item move on to someone else who will appreciate it more, so maybe it's time to think about whether you could let go of some of your own things.

Your outside environment will always be a reflection of what is going on for you on the inside. If your outside environment looks frazzled and cluttered, the best thing you can do is to take time to specifically appreciate everything that is within your range of vision and then send anything that you no longer need or love on its way with love and grace and appreciation to its next rightful custodian.

**Who you Are**

Think here about all your qualities and characteristics that make you special, and give appreciation for every single one of them. Who did you show up as today that made a positive difference in someone else's life? There will be at least one person who you have said or done something positive for today – even if you can't immediately think of it. And if you get tempted to look on any of your qualities as negative in some way, turn it around so that you find the positive intention and the goodness in that quality. For instance, if you tend to be a little impatient sometimes, this could also mean you have a passion for getting things done in a timely manner.

Also have appreciation for your body that has brought you successfully to where you are in your life so far. Be grateful for the fact you have your health in whatever way you have it. Be grateful for the limbs you have, the senses you have, and the fact that your heart continues to beat.

## What's Visible

When you are giving appreciation for everything you have in your life, remember to consider every aspect of what you have physically. Anything at all that you can see and touch deserves your thanks and gratitude. Turn your attention to all the little things you have experienced during your day so far such as fresh, clean water to drink in an endless supply, a comfortable and warm bed to sleep in and wake from, delicious food to eat and a table to sit at, as well as the bigger things like your house or the car you drive.

## What's Energetic

Here you are looking at everything else in your life that you cannot necessarily see or touch. So this is about experiences, emotions and things you can sense.

Search literally and specifically for events, situations, people, comments, anything at all from today, yesterday, the day before...

Use your senses and say out loud or to yourself specifically what you are grateful for such as, 'I am so grateful that I could sit in my garden and feel the gentle breeze on my face; I am so grateful for my mobility so I can walk in the fresh air when I choose, I am so grateful for the love I feel for my family and friends, and the love and support I get from them; I am so grateful for the smile the lady gave me when I walked past her in the street this morning; I am so grateful for my hearing so I can listen to and appreciate music and the sounds of nature; I am so grateful for....'

Say, 'Thank you Thank you Thank you' to the Universe, to your God, to Spirit, to Mother Nature – whomever and whatever makes sense to you and sits with your belief system – say the words out loud and repeat often.

# 'Appreciation'
# Quick Summary

Consider in the smallest detail what you H.A.V.E.™ in your life so you can appreciate...

And say 'Thank You'.

Often.

*"Every single successful person I've ever spoken to had a turning point and the turning point was where they made a clear, specific, unequivocal decision that they were not going to live like this anymore.*

*Some people make that decision at 15 and some people make it at 50 and most never make it at all."*

Brian Tracy

# CHAPTER SEVEN

## S.T.A.I.R.™ – Intention

The **I** in **S.T.A.I.R.™** stands for **Intention**. Setting an intention for yourself is like turning your compass to true north and walking steadfastly in that direction, ignoring any tempting diversions along the way, until you reach your destination. It's like setting the autopilot on an aeroplane – there really is only one end point of that journey, and it's at the destination that was set in advance.

Setting your intention for your day is a similar process. It is far more than simply setting a goal, writing it down and then hoping it might happen. It's a much deeper process that is almost visceral if you can connect in with it in a profound way. It's a felt experience far more than it is a cognitive process, such that it will influence every action you take because it will be the filter through which you experience your day.

As well as deciding what you want from your day, it's important to 'try on' what it will feel like when you have already achieved it. And then to intensify that feeling so your brain and your body have a 'dry-run' on your success and know what they are aiming for.

What exactly would you like to achieve from your day today?

Note this down in words or images in your journal, identifying at least 3 things if you can. Now take a good, long look at your journal entry – what do you notice about what you've just identified?

Does everything exist outside of you? 'External' to you?

Are they all things that involve you 'doing' something, such as sending those emails, sorting that pile, making that call, organising that space?

If that's the case, take a few more moments to identify some further additions to your list – that are 'internal' to you and relate to you as a human *being* not a human *doing*. For instance, is there a particular way you intend to be feeling by the end of the day? If you think carefully how you feel about yourself right at this moment, is that how you'd like to be feeling about yourself? If not, how would you like it to be different? What words would you use for how you would like to feel?

Are there any specific words you intend to speak during today? Is there a conversation you would like to set an intention of having today – perhaps a difficult one, or one you have been avoiding because it requires a depth of emotional investment and an open and honest dialogue? Is there someone you intend to say 'No' to today?

Setting your intention is a way to pre-plan your clear direction of travel. It will then act as a useful filter through which you make all your responses, take any actions or challenge any unhelpful thoughts and emotions that are keeping you stuck in a place where you'd rather not be.

You can set your intention about everything in your life, depending on wherever you find your challenges. Ask yourself a question and then write down your response in your journal as the clear intention you set for yourself today, for example:

What will I eat today? Today I will only eat healthy, nourishing food that supports my health and well-being.

How will I show up? Today I will show up as the calm, patient, compassionate me.

How slow or fast will I live through today? Today I will slow down long enough to spend some quality time with the people around me that matter.

When will I make time to just 'be' not 'do'? Today I will sit in the garden and rest for 30 minutes.

When will I take time out to meditate or show gratitude? Today I will spend at least 15 minutes in quiet gratitude and meditation.

What specifically do you want to be able to *say, do, feel or experience* by the end of today?

Who exactly are *you* going to show up as today?

Who would you choose? Which aspects of your personality get to have priority today? The stressed you with so little time? Or the relaxed, calmer you that sees joy in life and can find peace in all the chaos?

Are you willing to set that as your intention? Are you willing to honour your truth?

Are you willing to set your intention that today you will let go of your fear and give yourself permission to be authentic, to respond to any situation or circumstance intuitively, trusting your gut instinct?

Will you set your intention today to give yourself permission to say and be who you are authentically instead of hiding, for fear of being judged?

How, specifically, do you intend to be feeling during today and by the time you go to bed?

Can you set that as your intention?

For instance, 'Today, I will be feeling calm, grounded, confident, good about myself, valued, loved, appreciated......'.

Notice that no-one anywhere in any circumstance can 'make you feel' anything at all. It's a fallacy to think another person can control your emotions.

Your emotions and what you feel are an inside job – and you are always at a point of choice. You genuinely can choose to feel anything you want at any time (you just need to change the language you use with yourself on the inside).

So why wouldn't you set an intention that you are going to feel exactly as you'd like to feel?

Why wouldn't you set an intention that, today, things are going to be different, because today you are not going to be beholden to the negative barrage of self-criticism that is so familiar to you?

When you set your intention, you are deliberately setting an outcome for a point in time in the future, and your words will reflect that. For instance:

* by the end of today, I will be feeling grounded and calm;

* by the time I get up, I will be feeling refreshed and relaxed....

This is a deliberately different process to saying an affirmation which, as you know, is a positive statement made about you *in the present tense as though it is already true.* Setting your intention is about deliberately choosing a future state you intend to be in at a specific point in time, so the language changes accordingly.

# 'Intention'
# Quick Summary

Spend a few moments getting clear on exactly what you want from your day or by the time you get up. This is your compass, your direction of travel until you reach that future point in time.

What do you want to have achieved externally?

How do you want to be feeling internally?

How specifically do you want to be feeling about yourself?

Set your intention by saying, 'Today I will......'

*"We are not human beings having a
spiritual experience.*

*We are spiritual beings having a
human experience."*

Teilhard de Chardin

# CHAPTER EIGHT

## S.T.A.I.R.™ – Raise your Energy

The **R** in **S.T.A.I.R.™** stands for **Raise your Energy.**

Where are you in your body right now? Take a moment to pause and 'go inside' to see where it feels like you are. Are you in your head? Processing? Working things out? Deliberating? Re-running conversations and situations? Maybe you have a little analysis paralysis?

Or are you perhaps in the pit of your stomach? Feeling anxious about something? Or nothing? Ruminating over a conversation or situation? Or maybe responding to some internal self-criticism?

The most powerful resource you have available to you for raising your energy is the power of your imagination. This ability, used wisely and consciously for your own good, will change your life. Your brain is like a powerful computer, and you can programme it however you like. Some programmes will be useful and will move you towards the success and life you want, and others less so.

Research proves that you can achieve a similar level of successful results by mentally rehearsing a scenario or an outcome in your mind as you would if you were practising it for real. And this all comes down to your imagination and your power of visualisation, so you are now going to harness this energy and resource.

Wherever you are in your body, imagine that you can see yourself as a ball of vibrant energy. Notice any movement that you can see and whether there are any colours or sounds associated with your image. Now imagine yourself gently cradling your hands underneath it and, as you raise your hands slowly upwards, watch the ball of energy rise and along with it, your sense of where you are in your body to wherever feels comfortable.

This final step as you Climb your S.T.A.I.R.™ of Self-Confidence is all about consciously and deliberately raising your energy, both mentally and physically. There are several strategies that you can use to do this so try them all, and then practise and use whichever one(s) resonate most with you. As you work with any of the following visualisation techniques, you could also gently hold one hand in the other whilst pressing both your thumbs together and this will help to reinforce the new learning more holistically.

## ~ Altruism

Giving is receiving. Make altruism your new mantra and pay it forward. It feels so good to give something to another person or cause unconditionally, with no thought of wanting anything in return. Just because you can. What is the next thing you could 'give' in this way, and to whom?

## ~ Angel Wings

You do not need to believe in angels for this strategy to work. You simply need to allow your brain to create the images as powerfully as possible, and it will still have a positive effect and make a huge difference for you. Stand in front of a full-length mirror, or imagine yourself doing so if there isn't one available, and look at yourself. Let your gaze soften so that you take in the whole of you and your surroundings instead of looking at specific parts of your reflection. Now imagine that you see your Guardian Angel slowly walking up behind you; smiling, gentle, tall, strong, gracious and supportive. As your Guardian Angel reaches you, its light, soft wings of gold and white gently fold around you, first one which envelops the whole of your body, then the other which completes your sense of safety and security, and allows you to know that you are cared for and you are treasured. As the wings enfold you and support you, enjoy this moment and allow it to lift you up and let your spirit rise.

### ~ Breathe with the Tide

As you breathe in and breathe out imagine that your breath is an incoming tide. Be aware of where you are in your body right now, and with each in-breath raise your energy higher, and with your out-breath let it gently fall away, yet always closing higher than where it started. You mirror the movements of an incoming tide, which gently laps the beach, rising in slow, steady and incremental steps until it reaches its destination. Follow this movement until your energy is raised.

### ~ Feel Excited

You may not realise it fully yet, but you do have the ability to choose to feel anything you want to at any point in time. Your feelings are largely brought about by your thoughts and you can change your thoughts at any time. Did you also know that fear and excitement are 'two sides of the same coin' so they are very closely connected emotions?

Remember the last time you felt really, really excited? What was happening? Where were you? Who were you with? Take yourself back to that time right now. Recreate the experience for yourself in your mind. Recall as vividly as you can what it felt like to be really excited. Now intensify the feeling like turning up the dial on a cooker from simmering to boiling. Make it bigger. Move it somewhere more powerful in your body if necessary. Bring it closer to you if it feels too far away. Can you feel all the flutters in your tummy like a child at Christmas or on their birthday? Connect deeply with your experience of feeling that kind of excitement.

Be excited with a firm knowledge that something good is going to happen (what else do you have except the misery of telling yourself that 'life is awful and nothing good is ever going to happen'?) and take this bundle of energy and excitement and raise it up towards your heart and beyond, raise it up towards your Higher Self.

### ~ Future-Self Connection

Step into your own power and imagine that sitting in front of you is your future-self, an older version of you. However far into the future this person comes from is entirely up to you, but it is definitely you and it is definitely the you who has lived your life so far and has had all the experiences that you have had. They have also had all the experiences that you will have in the future. Just for now though, think of your future-self as someone else outside of you.

Watch as this person takes both of your hands in theirs, looks you in the eyes and gently says, 'I Love You', completely unconditionally.

Listen as they whisper, 'You Can Do This', whatever 'this' is that you want to achieve or create in this life.

They stay sitting with you, smiling with warmth, compassion and understanding in their heart.

They convey to you that you have the ability to achieve everything you want to in your life. It's already there before you. You just have to follow the steps.

As you bring your attention back to the present, see them still holding your hands as they come back with you, integrated and an essential part of you now, here, today. They are incorporated into you. Their wisdom, their knowledge, their essence.

## ~ Go In and Go High

Connect deeply with the force and energy of whatever you believe in that is bigger than you. Move the whole of your focus onto fully building this deeper sense of connection, then ask for help, support and guidance. Acknowledge to yourself that your God, the Universe, Spirit, Mother Earth, your Higher Self or whatever is relevant to you, wants you to succeed, wants you to live fully, wants you to experience being alive in the fullest, brightest way. Notice how good it feels, and how it raises your energy to become aware of this.

## ~ Golden Vessel

Imagine that your body is a vessel of some kind. You are still you. Your spirit is represented by a magical golden, sparkly elixir, full of energy and joy and movement. This is your essence. Picture this clearly and notice where the level sits within your body at the moment. Now watch as you pour more elixir in and watch the level rise higher and higher and higher until you feel a deep sense of connection and your spirit is raised.

## ~ Mexican Wave

Imagine that your body is covered with fur or feathers or some kind of fabric that has pile like velvet or velour. All of these textures have a comfortable way of lying so that if you stroke them one way, it feels really comfortable and smooth. Yet if you stroke it in the opposite direction, it would feel out-of-sorts like stroking a pet dog or cat 'the wrong way'. Imagine that the pile on your body is the 'right way' when it moves comfortably from your feet towards your head. Now visualise watching an upward movement of the pile like a Mexican wave from your feet to the top of your head. Let your energy rise with the rise of the crest of the wave.

### ~ Musical Moment

Music can be compelling, with the power to move you greatly; to lift you beyond your current reality and to create a whole new experience within the words and melody. That's why musical scores are so important in films. Find a piece of music that personally resonates with you in the most powerful way and that you passionately find motivating and inspiring. Maybe it stops you in your tracks, stirs you in the most profound way or brings you to tears because you connect with it so intensely. It might be an anthem, a ballad, a classical piece or whatever. Listen to it now either for real, or play it to yourself internally from memory. Connect with it as deeply as possible. As you listen; close your eyes, *feel* the music, connect with the tune and let each note lift you higher and higher.

## ~ Posture

Whether you are up and active through the day, or trying to sleep through the night, pay attention to your posture right now. Freeze frame it so you can observe it in great detail and notice what you would notice if you were outside of yourself.

What, if any, gestures are you currently making? What is your facial expression?

How and where are you holding any tension in your body? What's the positioning of your shoulders? Are they forward? Or drooped? Or raised uncomfortably high towards your ears constricting the area around your neck?

How are you holding your head? And more specifically, your chin? What position is it in? Is it low towards your chest? Or raised high? When you reflect objectively, are you holding any tension in your head area maybe around the back of your neck? This is a common area to hold tension without realising you are doing so.

What position are you holding your arms and legs in? Closed and crossed? Or open and free?

At times when you feel low in energy or self-esteem, you may find that you are holding tension in certain areas of your body, or holding yourself in certain positions that aren't supportive to you. A few simple changes can make a world of difference to how you feel. Sounds too simple? Give these easy movements to open up your body posture a try and notice what changes. Make each move slowly and thoughtfully so you can pay attention to the slightest shifts you experience. If you are using this particular strategy through the night trying to settle yourself back to sleep, you will need to adapt this slightly to ensure you stay horizontal.

Stand up with your feet shoulder-width apart and breathe in deeply and slowly whilst extending your arms horizontally out to the side like an aeroplane. Turn your palms upwards towards the sky. Close your eyes if it's comfortable and safe for you to do so, then on your next in-breath raise your chin slowly until you can feel a very slight stretch down your throat. Notice the energy rise and shift in your physiology.

A less obvious way to gain a similar benefit is to just simply lift your chin. Even a few centimetres will have a noticeable impact on how you feel in your body.

Your physiology will always reflect what is going on for you on the inside, and the process also works in reverse. So deliberately changing your posture on the outside will bring positive internal benefits too.

Always remember, wherever you are, to take the time to consciously look *up*. It's so easy to be in the habit of looking down or at eye level all the time. When did you last properly notice the architecture of the buildings you walk past every day? Make a decision to consciously look up to take in the full extent of your environment and to raise your own energy.

### ~ Rub Hands Together

You can generate vitality and warmth using a simple technique and then use this life-force to raise the energy in your body.

Rub your hands together briskly for at least 30 seconds until you feel a gentle tingle then place both hands over your heart.

At the same time imagine 'getting underneath' where you are in your body and gently nudging upwards. Feel the movement, degree by degree, as you raise your energy towards the warmth of your hands, towards your heart and on towards your Higher Self.

### ~ Swim Up to the Light

Imagine that you are swimming deep beneath the surface of the ocean, and you see the light of the sun above you. You see yourself swimming vertically towards the light, moving higher and higher towards the surface, the light getting brighter and brighter, until your head breaks through the surface and you breathe in deeply and feel the warmth of the sun on your face.

## ~ Twenty-Second Hug

Research now shows that if you hug another person for at least 20 seconds, your body will release enough of the feel-good hormone oxytocin to bring about real health benefits. And if you immediately follow that hug with 10 seconds of holding hands, the benefits are even greater. Most people do not hug for this length of time, probably only a few seconds, if that, so the benefits received are actually very limited. And as human beings, we need to have physical contact and connection so we can survive and thrive.

Renowned Psychotherapist Virginia Satir said, *"We need 4 hugs a day for survival. We need 8 hugs a day for maintenance. We need 12 hugs a day for growth."*

If it is feasible and appropriate, find someone you care about right now and ask them if it is OK to have a hug for 20 seconds. Connect fully along the length of your body, and agree with them that it's OK to stay like that for at least 20 seconds. Feel the transfer of energy between the two of you. Connect with their heartbeat and notice how it intertwines with yours.

Not only will this raise your own energy, it will also be a very beautiful and considerate gift to give the other person.

# 'Raise your Energy'
# Quick Summary

Notice where you are in your body, and see your essence as a ball of energy.

Use one of the strategies to raise your energy higher, through your body, towards your Higher Self.

Altruism

Angel Wings

Breathe with the Tide

Feel Excited

Future-Self Connection

Go In and Go High

Golden Vessel

Mexican Wave

Musical Moment

Posture

Rub Hands Together

Swim Up to the Light

Twenty-Second Hug

# JOINING ALL THE DOTS TOGETHER

If you have conscientiously and methodically worked through each step to Climb your S.T.A.I.R.™ of Self-Confidence you will have noticed a shift in your energy and in your areas of focus when you are going through a challenging time. You will have noticed a lessening in any feelings of anxiety, and you will be feeling better about yourself and more optimistic.

It can take a little time and practice to perfect the techniques. Give yourself praise for what you have managed to achieve so far, and allow yourself the opportunity to become even more skilled and fluent at applying each step.

Once you can move smoothly and gracefully through each step; Self-compassion; Time to pause, breathe and assess; Appreciation, Intention and Raise your energy, you will be able to reduce anxiety and re-balance your self-esteem in a matter of a few minutes. You will of course always have the choice and option to take a longer journey and move through each step in greater depth, and the choice will always be yours.

If you are having a particularly challenging time and, having completed all the steps feel like you need a little more, simply go back to the start and repeat all of the steps again in order, starting with the self-compassion affirmation. The effect of completing each step is cumulative, so the positive benefits will act like a layer upon layer of thinking and experiencing to bring you back to balance.

You may find it useful to see all the summaries from each chapter together, in order, for support whilst you practise and learn to Climb your S.T.A.I.R.™ of Self-Confidence  with ease, so here they are in the coming pages.

*If you happen to have jumped ahead straight to this part of the book, by all means use the opportunity to start learning each of the summaries but please ensure you go back and read the detail of each chapter so it makes complete sense through understanding the rationale and background to how each step came about and why it is relevant. You will then appreciate how each part interconnects and contributes to the whole.*

## 'Self-Compassion' Quick Summary

Always remember that, no matter what;

I am *loveable* and *capable*

I am *whole*, I am *unique*

I am *strong*, I am *resourceful*

I *matter*. I am *enough*.

# 'I am Loveable'
# Quick Summary

Step into the shoes of someone who adores you.

Stand in front of them and move position so you can see yourself through their eyes, with a filter of unquestionable, unconditional love.

See what *they* see, feel what *they* feel.

You are so loveable.

# 'I am Capable'
# Quick Summary

Whatever age you are right now,
you have already achieved so much
in your life. Either as a human-being or
human-doing. Pick one success and then
another and then another and identify
specifically what you had to do
to achieve that success.
You are so capable.

# 'I am Whole'
# Quick Summary

There is no part of you that is missing or
has to be found.
You are whole and complete.

## 'I am Unique'
## Quick Summary

The chances of you being born were 1 in $10^{2,685,000}$ which makes the fact of your existence a total miracle.

There is literally no-one else quite like you anywhere else in the world. You are completely unique and you are very, very special.

# 'I am Strong'
# Quick Summary

Think about a situation where you made
all the difference, where you dug deep
and did what needed to be done. Where
another person depended on you fully
and completely, and you came
through for them. Remember exactly
what it was that you said, or did, and
what you contributed to the situation.
You really are so very strong.

# 'I am Resourceful'
# Quick Summary

You have all the resources you need already inside you. Remind yourself of the qualities, skills, characteristics and traits you have and recall times when you have used creativity and flexibility in your approach to find a way forward when you have faced a problem or difficulty. Be grounded in the knowledge that you can choose to have a different relationship with any emotion you experience, at any time, simply by using your imagination and skills of visualisation. You can ask for what you need and you can get what you need.

# 'I Matter'
# Quick Summary

You have a right to be here. And you count.
You matter just as much as anyone else.
And you make a difference to the people
around you every single day.

# 'I am Enough'
# Quick Summary

**'I am now and I always will be enough.'**

# 'Time to Pause (to be Present)' Quick Summary

Make a decision to stop, even for just
a few moments, to allow yourself to
become fully grounded and be
present in the moment.
Connect with each of your senses
in turn – naming out loud everything
you can see, hear and touch.
Then everything you can smell and taste
(if relevant). Then connect with your
heartbeat and stay connected long
enough to appreciate
the joy of being alive.

# 'Time to Breathe (as you Body Scan)' Quick Summary

Consciously become aware of your breathing as you M.E.L.T.™[5] and complete a gentle Body Scan noticing what you notice, releasing all tension.

---

5. Make Everything Let go of Tension

# 'Time to Assess (the Arguments)' Quick Summary

Check out the arguments for and against what you are saying to yourself:

* Can you ask yourself a better question?

* Are you problem-focused or solution-focused?

* Is what you are saying to yourself 100% true, all of the time?

* How will you feel about this 5 years from now?

* What would your best friend say to you?

* What would you say if it was your best friend saying this to you?

# 'Appreciation'
# Quick Summary

Consider in the smallest detail what you
H.A.V.E.™ in your life so you can appreciate...

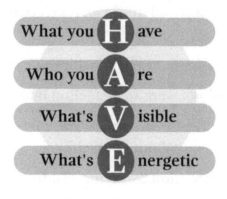

What you **H**ave

Who you **A**re

What's **V**isible

What's **E**nergetic

And say 'Thank You'.

Often.

# 'Intention'
# Quick Summary

Spend a few moments getting clear on exactly what you want from your day or by the time you get up. This is your compass, your direction of travel until you reach that future point in time.

What do you want to have achieved externally?

How do you want to be feeling internally?

How specifically do you want to be feeling about yourself?

Set your intention by saying, 'Today I will......'

# 'Raise your Energy' Quick Summary

Notice where you are in your body, and see your essence as a ball of energy.

Use one of the strategies to raise your energy higher, through your body, towards your Higher Self.

Altruism

Angel Wings

Breathe with the Tide

Feel Excited

Future-Self Connection

Go In and Go High

Golden Vessel

Mexican Wave

Musical Moment

Posture

Rub Hands Together

Swim Up to the Light

Twenty-Second Hug

# Climb your

## S.T.A.I.R.™ of Self-Confidence

**S**elf-Compassion

I am *loveable* and *capable*
I am *whole*, I am *unique*
I am *strong*, I am *resourceful*
I *matter*. I am *enough*.

**T**ime

to

Pause (and be Present)
Breathe (as you Body Scan)
Assess (the Arguments)

**A**ppreciation

**I**ntention

**R**aise your energy

# WHAT NEXT?

The **Spirit Level Success™ System – Six Secrets of Self-Esteem** is a complete system and each Secret is a core component of what I believe needs to be in balance to maintain a healthy, robust core and feel good about yourself all the time – no matter what is going on in your life.

**Secret #1** gets you there; **Secrets #2 – #6** keep you there.

Wherever 'there' is for you.

The most important relationship you will ever have in your life is with yourself. If you don't feel good about yourself, if you are lacking in self-acceptance, if you are constantly struggling to like who you are then this will contaminate every other relationship you have in your life. So coming back to a healthy and wholesome sense of self, and giving yourself the tools to be able to do so literally any time you need to, is one of the biggest gifts you can give yourself.

You may have already experienced some important shifts in your perception and how you feel about yourself as you spent time and progressed step by step through this book. Hopefully you have implemented all the steps in the right order, and have noticed a difference in how you are able to turn things around in circumstances where before, you may have spiralled into repetitive, unhelpful thinking patterns.

How would you like to build on this work and safeguard those shifts for the future, so they move from being fragile and easily forgotten, to something embedded in your personal toolkit of emotional and psychological survival and longevity?

How would you like to ensure that you continue to build a sustainable, robust ability to reduce anxiety and re-balance your self-esteem and sense of self-worth any time, *every time*, whenever you need it to manage fear or self-criticism, self-doubt or anxiety, in a healthy, sustainable way?

To gain the depth of insight and understanding needed to really make the sustainable shift you so want, and to continue your journey to lasting and robust inner confidence, please visit www.spiritlevelsuccess.com to gain access to all six Secrets which I invite you to progress through in the online and live coaching programmes.

# ACKNOWLEDGEMENTS

I would like to thank everyone who has helped me along the road to writing this book and creating and developing the Spirit Level Success™ System – Six Secrets of Self-Esteem (www.spiritlevelsuccess.com), which is my way of giving something back to the world and of leaving my legacy.

Without the insights, depths, reflections and experiences gained over a lifetime and, more specifically, in the two years during which this programme came alive, this book may never have been written.

So I would like to say a huge thank you to the following people;

To my husband Lee for never wavering in your love for me and for your faith in what you always knew I would be able to achieve. For standing side by side with me through everything I have experienced in my life and always backing me, no matter what. You really are my rock and best friend.

To my daughters, Ellie and Ruby, for teaching me the beauty and gift of unconditional love, for your laughter, for your smile and for making our family what it is.

To my accidental mentor, Ian Lawman. Ian, your wisdom, guidance, stamina and motivation have helped make all this possible. You have been integral to my success, and I would not be where I am today with Spirit Level Success™ if it wasn't for you, and your generosity of time, energy and enthusiasm.

I would like to thank my parents, Valerie and Patrick, and my brother Gary and his family for always being there for me and for loving me.

Thanks also to my dear friend, confidante and spiritual soul sister, Julie Anne Hart. I look forward to so many more of our chats together, our deepening connection and our hysterical laughter.

I'd like to thank my incredibly talented friend Trevor Folley, whose feedback after reading my first piece of work, my digital book *You Are Enough* brought me to tears and made me believe in myself even more and realise that maybe I really did have something special to contribute to the world.

To my team at Spirit Level Success™ without whom this book would not have happened – thank you for everything –

Publisher, Sarah Houldcroft (www.goldcrestbooks.com)

Designer, Gail Bradley (www.gailbradleydesign.co.uk)

Technical Guru, Sue Mitchell (www.bluebellbusinessservices.com)

And finally, to say a huge thank you for anyone in my life so far who has given me any kind of **G.I.F.T.**™[6] along the way – whether or not you are still present, and whether or not you know it, I couldn't have created this without you.

---

6. Golden Insight into Feelings and Thoughts

# ABOUT THE AUTHOR

Bernadette Sarginson is a former lawyer turned Empowerment Coach and Mentor who is an Intuitive with a mission. That mission is to assist as many people as possible to really own and acknowledge their true unlimited potential and unique place in the world, so that they can live their most magnificent life possible and make the difference they came here to make. She has successfully coached and mentored hundreds of individuals and groups through long term change management and personal development.

Working in a bespoke and unique way, she brings a powerful mixture of life experience, intuitive wisdom, education and coaching to her work to enable you to raise your game both personally and professionally.

On the inside, Bernadette spent years suffering from social anxiety, feeling like her self-esteem had deserted her much of the time, and with overwhelming self-doubt. Yet on the outside she had a bubbly personality, and professional success.

The **Spirit Level Success™ System – Six Secrets of Self-Esteem** is the result of over 30 years of reflection, insight and wisdom and is guaranteed to reduce anxiety, and re-balance your self-esteem and sense of self-worth – any time, every time.

She lives near Melton Mowbray in the United Kingdom with husband Lee and their daughters, Ellie and Ruby.

Secret #1 – Self – where you **Climb your S.T.A.I.R.™ of Self-Confidence** is part of the **Spirit Level Success™ System – Six Secrets of Self-Esteem** and you can access resources and find out more about the complete system at www.spiritlevelsuccess.com.

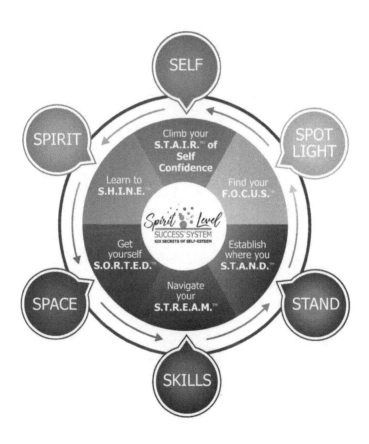

My Journal